Country Matters

Country Matters

IAN NIALL

Illustrations by Donald Watson

LONDON
VICTOR GOLLANCZ LTD
1984

These articles originally appeared in
Country Life from 1953 onwards.

First published in book form
in Great Britain 1984
by Victor Gollancz Ltd,
14 Henrietta Street, London WC2E 8QJ

British Library Cataloguing in Publication Data
Niall, Ian
   Country matters.
   1. Country life—Great Britain—History—
   20th century
   2. Natural history—Great Britain
   I. Title
   941.082′092′4   S522.G7

ISBN 0-575-03521-8

Typeset by Centracet
and printed in Great Britain by
St Edmundsbury Press, Bury St Edmunds, Suffolk

Author's Note

I look at these pieces written for *Country Life* over a period of 34 years and suffer a recurrence of a lifelong complaint, nostalgia for 'a world I never made' but which was there when I came into it as a child in Galloway. Reading again the minor essays and character studies I was encouraged to do for the three editors I have known, Frank Whitaker, John Adams and Michael Wright, I am aware of two significant facts: that I was blessed in being allowed to write whatever I had a mind to write and have it published, and that I was happy doing something I loved doing, for few people these days can say as much. Being happy and making others happy is what life should be about. Many readers of *Country Life* have written to me over the years suggesting that my 'specials' might appear in book form. I hope they enjoy some of the 400 I wrote in these years, selected carefully by my friend and publisher, David Burnett of Victor Gollancz, and illustrated by another gifted friend, Donald Watson, who long ago had the good sense to settle in the country of my infant nurture, Galloway, and had visited that part of North Wales in which I lived for 40 years.

Ian Niall
Ashley Green, Bucks

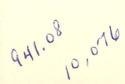

Contents

Country Matters

Memories of a White Christmas

We haven't had a white Christmas since we came to live in our present house in North Wales, largely because snow doesn't stay long at the worst of times, owing, they say, to the salt in the air. Our last white Christmas was when we were in our old village in 1956, I think it was. I know it took the village by surprise one grey afternoon when flocks of birds had been passing over steadily for two hours or more and the last flight of the starlings had gone like leaves in a gale, swinging and dipping and rushing on into the darkening heavens. There was no wind and no sunset. I enjoyed playing at being a weather prophet. Mark my words, I said, aping my grandfather when he made this kind of observation, snow is on the way. Those who didn't want snow looked at me in disgust. Those who hang on anyone's gloomy prediction nodded their heads. 'Them birds know a thing or two,' they said.

I wasn't surprised when it began to snow almost immediately as dusk settled about us. It lined the upper sides of the branches of trees across the road in the glen. It hung on walls and gateposts, and anyone with half an eye could tell it would be there in the morning. I looked at the stream in the glen. It had stopped bubbling and frothing and flowed black and glassy in the gloom. It was going to freeze, and we were two days from Christmas Eve. In the darkness I carried some logs to the back door and stacked them there and took three or four in to stand them on

11

the hearth. The snow they had gathered made pools of water on the hearth stone, and the logs steamed. For the remainder of the evening I enjoyed being snug indoors. I put my feet up and played at listening to the silence—everything that moved in the village was insulated, and its sounds were muffled. I looked out before I went to bed. I could hear the sea. Even the waves had a different sound. The wind was creeping up and blowing a chilling breath of the north-east on to the already considerable blanket of snow.

In the morning the whole world was white. Up on the slopes above the village things stood out as they had never done before—a black steer foraging round an iron trough, a fallen tree back-lit by the snow, and a dog going uphill to a huddle of sheep under a bank and a tall hedge. People plodded down from the farms, beat their arms on their flanks and agreed we were set for a white Christmas. They said that up in their part of the world the cold wind would cut a man's ears off. Water troughs were frozen, so they were having to carry water to the cattle. The streams were frozen too. The hill down into the village was glazed. Cars weren't getting up, but the reckless ones from the back country were coming down, careering and bumping and sliding. Those who had walked down shrugged their shoulders about the others who had come in cars. What went up must come down, they said, but what came down might not go up again and be left to freeze solid over Christmas.

The novelty of a white Christmas was wearing off. People quickly lose their enthusiasm for the picturesque scene when they have slipped and slid and trampled through snow for an hour or two. They get tired quickly when snowballs form on their boots. Even a return to the fireside takes their energy away. As far as I was concerned, I had had enough of it because I saw only misery for the redwings sheltering in the canopy of laurels and rhododendrons across the way. The movement of starlings made me shiver. The background of the sky was like a Siberian scene depicted by a landscape artist. Birds from the shore flew over in trailing groups, looking over the country for a place where they could feed on softer ground, but finding none.

I have never been able to stand being cooped up for very long, and on Christmas Eve, with tradesmen drifting about, delivering stale bread for stuffing, sausage meat, chestnuts—everything, it seemed, but kippers and fresh strawberries and cream, I took less comfort from being confined than I might have done at any other time. I went and found my cartridge belt, the gun and bag, and slipped out. I had no dog, but a dog would have suffered in the deep snow. I told myself they would be glad to see me go.

12

I went up the hollow, studying the tracks in the snow, and when a hare got up from the side of the stream I shot him. There was a penalty in doing so for I had condemned myself to carrying his 8 lb. all the rest of the way, unless I left him there and retraced my steps to get him. I went on, remembering another day in the snow when I made a mixed bag, and soon I came up with a wigeon that had been down along the edge of the frozen stream. I was surprised. Wigeon aren't as common on small waters as mallard or teal. Along a frozen stream I hardly expected to find one, but all sorts of unusual things happen when the land freezes up and is covered with snow. A heron had been stalking along the stream, finding nothing, it seemed to me, until it had stopped and speared into some grass, catching some small animal perhaps and leaving no more tracks to be followed. In a stretch of frozen bog where the round rushes stuck up as stiff and stark as spines on a porcupine I was startled by a snipe getting up almost at my feet. I shot it when it was far out. It was a jack-snipe and pathetically small. My conscience began to be troubled as I stood turning it over in my hand. I really hadn't much excuse for carrying home a hare or a snipe. The larder was well-stocked with more meat than we could eat without getting bloated. I looked down at the village, seeing the dark corrugations on the roads and the smoke rising. People were still hurrying about getting mistletoe at the last minute, a bigger roasting tin, a holly wreath, laying in stores as though threatened by a siege; and everything was emphasised by the fact that a white Christmas was upon us, giving a strange throw-back picture of the isolation experienced by man in the dim past.

Partridges were in the field where the sheep had cropped down the kale. I heard one call and went down there, but they filed away as I entered the field at the top end, vanishing into the hedge at the bottom, leaving a trail and an odd feather. I stood where they made their exit and saw Hughie, who had been out foraging for holly, coming towards me. He didn't want the hare for his dog. The snipe looked too much like a sparrow to be offered to anyone. I didn't offer to buy his holly, though he turned it round and round to make the most of its blighted, hard little berries; and, that being that, he hurried on across country to try to sell it at the inn in the village on the top of the hill. As he went he put up a hare that galloped straight back towards me, coming head-on and oblivious to my being in its path, but I waved my arms and shouted and it turned. Hughie looked back and waved hesitantly, not knowing what it was about. I had abandoned the idea of making a mixed bag and, in any case, was beginning to think about the warmth of the fire, the snugness one appreciates more when the day is wearing away and

13

the snow crystallises under one's feet, glazing in places where there was a slight thaw.

I passed the cattle shelter on the way down. It had been open to the wind, and the snow had drifted in. Someone had been up to inspect it and had gone away again to fetch a bale of hay, but there were no cattle there. They were where they had gone at the onset of the snow, away down to the bottom corner of the field, all standing together, forlornly waiting for night, chewing on turnips that had been scattered for them. They seemed to think that I was bringing something more appetising for them to eat and began to come towards me in a jostling procession until I turned off and went through the footpath gate leading down to the glen stream. The banks of the stream were clothed in fragments of ice that had broken away in the force of the main current and piled themselves over obstructions in their path.

I straightened the dead hare and hung it in the outhouse along with the snipe and stamped my feet before going indoors. The gun had to be cleaned before I warmed myself with rum, and, when I looked out at the garden, the snow seemed slightly grey, but the hedges looked blacker than before. There was no doubting now that it would be white on Christmas day.

The snow was there in the morning, but we didn't see much of the outside world: the windows steamed up, and the sky lowered to a sort of dull yellow. The postman's helpers blew into their cupped hands and then hurried on to get finished. The last church-goer plodded up through the snow and disappeared, and the feeling of being insulated from the cold and everything outside was complete.

We had our white Christmas, our chiming bells and nostalgia-making carols, a surfeit of mince-pies and cold turkey. I am not sure now whether we ate the hare or gave it away to someone who had a revulsion against cold turkey. It thawed on Boxing night, I think, to everyone's relief.

An Old Farm Kitchen

Early recollections are often most vivid, because they concern what are called one's impressionable years. If I think of my own I am immediately transported to the kitchen of my grandfather's house, for it was there that I took my first steps, having been sent to the country as an infant in

14

the belief that country air and country food were essential for my survival. It turned out, of course, that I was far from frail. I grew and flourished like the green bay tree and there was no need for any molly-coddling at all, assuming that there was time for pampering in so busy a household.

There may have been times when an impression was made on me by the solemn, steady tick of the grandfather clock and the impatient buzzing of a bluebottle trying to escape at the window, but more often than not that farmhouse kitchen was as busy as the stackyard at threshing, the 20-acre in the heat of harvest or the hayfield that, in those far-off days, had to be turned by lines of men plying wooden rakes like beings possessed, especially when the far-away mountain was half-obscured by lowering cloud.

If my grandfather held sway everywhere beyond the porch, and was ritually master at the head of the table, it was my grandmother who ran things within the threshold, and her industry and organisation set the pace for everything outside. There could be no threshing without baking, cooking, brewing and churning, and no one could rise early to harvest unless at some time or other grandmother had prepared for that breakfast, salting a ham, making preserve, laying in stores. The town was a considerable distance away and it would have been a shame and a disgrace, in any case, had the humblest labourer been asked to eat anything that was not home-baked. It would have indicated a sad state of indolence had the soda-bread been buttered with anything but butter churned in the dairy across the court. To provide porridge for the man who had to be warm in order to go to the far marches to bring down a ploughing team, the pot had to be constantly on the hob and there had to be someone to stir the pot.

In the corner of the kitchen there stood an article of furniture called an ark. It was, in fact, a sort of bunker that held one quarten sack of oats and one of flour. Tea and sugar had to be stocked in similar proportions: a chest of tea, a sack of flour. The ham that hung on the ceiling hooks was salt and those who had it for breakfast needed copious amounts of tea to quench their thirst. They needed tea at breakfast time and tea in the mid-morning.

Two, or sometimes three, baskets had to be prepared and tea cans filled to be carried to the men who might be working in two or three different places. Pancakes were baked for the tea baskets, pancakes and oven scones.

Large quantities of gooseberry jam, black-currant and blackberry jam were laid in at the appropriate season. For a good part of the late

15

summer and early autumn half of the burnished iron range was taken up by the brass preserving pan. The labour in the kitchen matched the labour out of doors.

As soon as the mid-day meal was cleared away—as many as six men and sometimes more had to be fed with broth or soup, potatoes, mutton, salt beef or boiled ham, followed by whatever sweet would fill them full—the womenfolk began to prepare for their orgy of baking.

Mounds of soda scones, treacle scones and scones made of potato or oatmeal were turned out and left to cool under a white linen cloth. It used to puzzle me as a small child how unconcerned the baking woman was to see so much of her labour devastated when the first wave of workers came from the harvest field to eat before lending a hand at milking.

The clock ticked, but no one heard it, except perhaps myself when the house was all at once empty, and my aunts were off somewhere in the garden picking a black-currant bush, or gathering gooseberries or apples.

I cannot think of the farm kitchen when it did not have some mouth-watering, appetising scent about it. Even when my grandmother was making mushroom ketchup the spices had a delicious aroma. Time was all she lacked, good housekeeper that she was; time to deal with a newly-slaughtered pig—she wasted nothing but the grunt—time to pickle and salt things, to make brawn, to lay up fat carefully clarified, to label and pack away every storable thing that would provide for a day to come, to make shortbread that melted in one's mouth, blackberry wine that tasted like port, and even nettle beer to clear the blood of impurities.

It seems to me that even with time so precious there was time for certain ritual, for the brass tap on that monster of iron that was called a range was polished until it shone like gold, and so did the rail, the mantel-rail that enclosed the inevitable brass candlesticks which, in my innocence, I really took to be gold until grandmother had gone to her long home and someone remarked that the brass candlesticks had lost a little of their brilliance through neglect and that the old lady would not rest easy if she thought that things were not being kept as she had kept them for a lifetime.

The pressure on the kitchen hardly ever seemed to diminish. When harvest was over and the business of laying away fruit, preserves and all the surplus of summer and autumn was over there would surely be a threshing on a large scale. We had our own mill but it wasn't adequate. When large quantities of straw and grain were urgently needed, the steam threshing mill would be summoned to enable the first stock of

16

grain to be put in the granary and the strawhouse to be filled for bedding the wintering cows.

The mill men were fed along with our own workers and whatever neighbours came to lend a hand.

When at length the threshing ended and the mill engine sat cooling down in the stackyard, at nightfall there was a social occasion, a sort of second harvest home, a supper of roasted spare ribs, or a hare that had been shot on the stubbles, cheese from the great tub cheese that stood on the corner of the table so that anyone could cut for himself and replace the 'lid' or crust. This was another thing that grandmother had to watch.

Although there was nothing about cheesemaking that she did not know, we no longer made cheeses, and the buying of cheese was something to which some thought had to be given. In a dairying countryside people were judged by the quality of the cheese they had on their table. It had to be of exactly the right flavour, crumble as a good cheese should, and keep as no cheese will keep nowadays.

When I think about it, my grandmother must have been a most careful woman. She wasted nothing, she anticipated every need of the household. Ask her for anything from a clove to a section of honey and she could produce it, and she still found time to see that the range was burnished, the parlour fire built with peats, and honeysuckle gathered from the hedge to drench the back porch with sweet scent at nightfall.

If someone came into the kitchen with a pheasant that had been beheaded by the reaper she had the bird hung. If they brought her a hare she bled it for soup. At daybreak she would be picking over mushrooms gathered on the old turf of the field behind the house, and last thing at night, by the light of the oil lamp, she would be stitching another square in her patchwork quilt, or making toddy for someone who had stayed too long in a downpour.

Things have changed beyond recognition, and I doubt whether many farm kitchens today are stocked with a crate of tea, a side of bacon, sacks of sugar, oat and flour. I am sure there are not many where every loaf or cake is baked at home. Some of those cakes were made from secret recipes and had as many as two dozen eggs in them. The deep freeze, the travelling shop, the refrigerator and the washing machine have revolutionised the life of the farmer's wife and transformed her kitchen from a place of burnished steel, shining brass and copper and hard labour, to enamel, bright chrome and comparative ease.

I have no doubt that my grandmother would have loved these things, but I have a feeling that she would still have put her salt hams on the hooks, stored away her ketchup and jams and jellies, and laid in enough stores to withstand a month-long siege, for this was the housekeeping she learned as her mother's hand-maid.

The burnished metals were the symbols of industry, and nothing in life must be wasted—the little yellow apple on the most gnarled tree in the garden, the berry on the bush or the passing minute that was recorded by the steady ticking of the wag-at-the-wall clock.

The High-stepper

My mother's family were mainly seafaring men. My father's kept their feet firmly on dry land, and the horse was to them what a cross-Atlantic clipper was to my maternal side.

Unpretentious in almost everything else they did, father's family were inordinately proud of their way with horses. Every horse they possessed was one of the family, but they were never sentimental about animals. They respected horses as noble creatures in their own right. Every horse the family owned was therefore a character, not the least of them the high-stepping trotter grandfather acquired the year I was born.

One of my earliest recollections is that of posing to have my photograph taken with my father, grandfather and great-grandfather. I was the only one not wearing a watch and chain with an ornament dangling from the fob, for I was only three years old. I remember coming into town at a spanking pace, the four generations of us sitting upright in the gig. I was the only one without a hard hat, and Tammy the pony flicked his ears at the sound of my voice. We travelled like the wind.

Soon afterwards I made another memorable journey in the gig. It was to meet my mother, who had come down to visit my grandparents and see how they were bringing up a first-born son too delicate for the foul air of the city. That day was memorable, not because I was re-united with my mother, but because the famous trotter did his best to unload us over a bridge on to the very train that had brought mother down from Glasgow to Galloway.

The pony had waited rather long for the train to arrive. When it did, and mother was safely aboard, he headed for home at a cracking pace. The train, making its departure for places farther along the Wigtownshire Railway, passed under the bridge at the precise moment that the pony reached the middle of the bridge, and the train-driver thoughtlessly blew the whistle. Tammy, a most high-spirited, fine-legged, sleek animal, reared up immediately and pawed the air with his forefeet, threatening to bring them down on the wrong side of the parapet. He was hauled from the brink but threatened to tip us all out over the parapet on the other side of the road. Mother and I fell into the well of the gig and were immediately lost in a jumble of travelling rugs. Tammy was persuaded to come down on all fours.

As soon as he had done this the terrified pony set out for home at such speed that for a while it seemed we might even pass the departing train, but the tail light of the train diminished. People in the village we passed through came out to see what was amiss, summoned by the drumbeat of the pony's hooves and the sound of showering grit spurting from our wheels.

Mother hadn't quite recovered her cool when the lathered pony drew up in the steading of the farm. She thought grandfather had been showing off, or even trying to frighten her. How was she to know that this hard-mouthed pony went at his own pace, like the well-known bat out of hell, set his ears back, listened to no one, and liked it best when he could take the gig round a tight bend, one wheel rising a foot off the ground? She was not to know that this was the horse of the family's life. They loved him. As far as they were concerned, he was the fastest horse in the world.

Tammy was entered for every trotting race promoted in that part of the world, and, believe it or not, he was never beaten, even in old age. I think it was something to do with his nature. He could not bear to be passed by anything on the road or a grass track.

He was almost a trotting machine. He held his head high with his neck beautifully arched. Whoever rode him simply had to sit there like a monkey. His rhythm was perfection, and I am sure the family would not have taken a thousand pounds for him. The few bookies to be found in remote places in those days quickly put up the bar against Tammy. People who had pride withdrew their ponies when he was entered, or wanted him handicapped, which never made the slightest difference.

I rode him once, down to the smithy for a set of trotting shoes, but we never got there. My hat fell off and I foolishly turned his head for home. Alas, he wouldn't slow down so that I could pick up my hat. He didn't slow down for a five-bar gate, but somehow broke the trot to clear it. My chin came in contact with his head, which was very hard. Tears came to my eyes and blood from my nose. We went all the way back to the stable door at a fast trot. I dismounted, wiped away my tears, rubbed my bloody nose, and walked him all the way to the smithy and back.

Tammy scared me again, later, when he took off as we drove an Irish

19

harvester to catch the boat train. The gig hit an iron gate that hung across the road, its hitch rope having come adrift. We didn't see the obstruction as we passed from a moonlit patch of road into the shadows of an ash tree. I remember the pony going and I remember him skidding on his heels to pull up at the picket fence a few minutes before the train came in.

There was one last race before his master died, and he won that too, at the age of 20. My aunt led him down the road as far as the march gate when the old man's long funeral procession of cars set off for the kirk and the graveyard. Afterwards she led him back, and he went out to pasture for good, pensioned off.

The Day of the Pony

Although it must have been obvious to anyone with a little foresight that the motorcar was taking over and the sweet, sickly smell of petrol would mark its trail across the most remote stretch of moorland, no one in the world of my childhood faced that fact. The law no longer required a man with a red flag to walk in front of the motor. It came on like an unescorted bull. Its big brass headlamps may have blinked, but it wasn't very nocturnal and its daytime stare was arrogant. When Great Uncle Charlie got himself a car it was grudgingly admired. He would end up in the ditch, of course. It would run away with him on a hill. It was an inhuman thing and didn't respond to verbal command as a pony did. He had joined the nuisances on the road, the travelling threshing machines, the steam dragons belching smoke and spewing cinders, and moreover, he was aspiring to grandeur. One day he would exchange his whipcord britches for motoring tweeds, put on great gauntlets and a scarf round his neck and come home and milk his fine Ayrshire herd in gloves!

Great Uncle Charlie did none of these things, but he didn't really win reapproval when he took a calf to market in his fine tourer, albeit clothed in a sack tied at the animal's neck. How much faster did he get along the road, anyway, with all his noise and fuss when the road to market was busy with traffic—farmers in their gigs, to say nothing of cattle being driven? What would he have done with the time he thought he could save? He parked his car in isolation. Old farmers who left their ponies in the mews came and looked it over and pondered what the levers and clocks were about. Small boys swarmed over it, and Great Uncle Charlie was no better off than the man who came to market and paid someone to hold his pony while he did his business or supped his ale. He, too, had to pay a sixpence to have someone act as guardian to his new conveyance. Almost certainly that town lounger let his friends inspect the car, perhaps taking a penny a time.

Whatever the farming community thought of Great Uncle Charlie and the odd farmer here and there who had more money than sense and bought a motorcar, the reaction of the family wavered between pride and disdain. Great Uncle Charlie occasionally came visiting on a Sunday and everyone came out to see him arrive. He handled the car with a certain self-consciousness that sprang from the feeling that he was a renegade. I believe he tried to back it as though he had a gig or a four-in-hand. But he never looked right in a gig after that.

In time he was accepted as a motorist. The family confessed that they owned him; he was one of us. It had to be said, but it was said as though he had been an alcoholic or not quite right in the mind. We remained faithful to the pony. The pony and trap took us everywhere. It, too, could transport a calf to market, and often did. It took us to the shore for picnics, to the village for those small items never kept in bulk at home, to the cattle show and to church. It wasn't grand, but it was dignified and dignity was something to be preserved as grandeur was to be disdained. The farmers who had cars were so few and far between that they never got much chance to race one another to and from market. A gig might cut ruts on the roadside bank and spill its passengers in the hedge and no one said much about it, but when the car came to grief news spread as though the fiery cross had been carried.

A friend of grandfather's had the misfortune to end up in the ditch with grandfather a passenger in his new motor, and the old man came home shaken and shaking his head as he vowed never to have a thing that couldn't be turned away from danger, a spluttering monster that dug itself in and wore itself out until it was as useless as a horseless cart.

The cars came on, of course. Not all of them were high, long-bonneted and grand. Mr Ford and one or two others were making them less ornate and a little cheaper, although that didn't impress us very much. There had been a certain quality about the coachwork of the first of them, a solidity about those brass lamps and heavy doors. Now we seemed to be in for the equivalent of the tinker's cart. The pony and gig, turned out well-groomed and shining, made such self-propelled 'henhouses' look tawdry. We would not have a car. No one bothered to say that there was the slightest touch of sour grapes or even sadness about it, but farming prices were low and only the extravagant fellow trying to show off spent his money on such things. It was true that a pony ate corn while it did nothing, but it didn't need spare parts and there were invariably shoes for its feet.

The more certain the revolution in transport became the tighter we clung to the pony and gig. On the road we drew to the side to let the noisome things pass, and travelled between times at a proper pace to see the corn growing and the rooks on the turnip hill. We sang songs and could hear ourselves sing. We stopped at the springs and the mossy water troughs along the way to let the happy pony take great draughts of water. We loved the jingle of harness, the sound of iron-shod wheels churning the road-side grit.

Our world was being changed by the 'tarmen', however. These black-faced fellows had taken the place of the stone-breaker, who since time immemorial had filled the potholes of green-tracked, metalled roads. Now they were covering hills with tar and patching and mending in places where the fume of bitumen took the place of the scent of myrtle and meadowsweet. Worse than this, the glassy surface often made the pony's feet slip. We cursed them as we did the motorcar. They and their dirty work were by-products of the age of the automobile.

As more and more country people took to the car it was noticed that the pony and gig was looked upon with a degree of curiosity. It was as though grandfather had gone back to wearing his tall hat to church (it was reserved for funerals by this time). When we stopped in the village small boys and elderly people would come out to speak to the pony and offer him a slice of bread with butter and sugar, the old ones sensing that the day of the gig was over and the younger ones fascinated by the novelty of four or five people travelling in such a manner.

Time had eroded the family's determination to have nothing to do with the motorcar. Even grandfather talked of getting one 'one day'. That day was far off, however. This much had to be understood. A time would come when the gig would wear out. The pony would have to be put to pasture in his old age. Then, perhaps, grandfather would have a motorcar. The pony was groomed and looked after with as much care and affection as ever. The gig had never been washed and polished quite so often. Woe betide the hens that perched upon it in the open-sided shed!

The motor car never supplanted the pony and gig. Grandfather's last pony survived him. He and grandmother both went to their final resting places by motor hearse. I sometimes wonder how they explained this to their ancestors, for the age of the horse had lasted more than a thousand years.

A Witch in the Family

Although I cannot recall exactly when I first heard about old Nan, I know it was a long time ago. She is one of the skeletons in our cupboards and I bring her out now as a sort of warning to those who have an urge to explore their family tree. My own forbears were here a while before the Normans came, but somewhere between then and now—I haven't the papers by me—was Nan. I had one great-uncle by the name of Peter who explored the records to find whether we came from the Ancient Kings of Ireland—an amazing number of Celts do—or whether we were first heard of hurrying back from Derby in '45 with as many cattle as we could drive. He was an honest man, great-uncle Peter. It was only when he had a glass of toddy in him that he went as far as to claim the Ancient Kings. Most of the time he admitted that he had no proof that we had ever set foot in Ireland, but he wasn't so sure about sheep-stealing and cattle-raiding. He said nothing when he discovered the positive proof that old Nan was back there among the obscure generations, for everyone knew already that Nan had been a witch.

A family can't have a witch in it without heredity taking a hand in subsequent generations. We laugh about Nan. We point her out when we recognise her in female relatives, but, on the whole, she's a family secret. It wouldn't do to let everyone know all about Nan, Nan as she was in her day and as she is now, drifting among us with her uncanny gifts. Some of us deny that she was a witch and try to discredit the whole story. The odd thing about it is that the discrediting faction have most of her gifts.

My grandfather laid down the law about Nan. He said the whole thing was a 'damned lie' invented by his brother as a counterblast to one of his own stories. I should make it plain here that the story-tellers among us were jealous of the position of top man and there may be a little truth in grandfather's claim that Nan's gifts were mainly the product of his brother's imagination, but nevertheless Nan existed. She was red-headed, six-feet-three in height and, to make things worse, she was double-jointed. She farmed. Her husband farmed too. Perhaps she was the only great character among the females of the family. All the others were known as 'the wife of James,' 'the wife of Charles' or 'the wife of John.' It amuses me that I cannot recall the name of the husband of Nan. Had he been of any consequence his name would surely have come to me, but he is no more than a vague shadow while great, broad-shouldered, double-jointed Nan stalks through her time, a virago, a character, a witch!

Nan, according to my grandfather's salty way of putting things, was 'a big woman fit to wrestle an ox or put a man under her arm.' He denied her powers, but filled in the details of her life with all the imagination at the family's command. The nearest picture I had of the witch—I am among the believing faction—was that of my grandfather's sister, who was tall and not unlike a man in some ways, although she had a heart of gold and cast no spells to my knowledge. In fact, my great-aunt was short of six feet in height. Her hair was black and she was not double-jointed, but for some reason she was the foundation for my vision of old Nan and I was a little in awe of her when she came to visit us, for she had the eyes of the witch.

People who had witnessed the hasty temper of some of the family often remarked that the eyes of the angry ones flashed. It was old Nan looking out. When that happened one could expect that somewhere in the distance there would be a rumble of thunder, that the milk would turn and the sun bury itself in a black cloud. No one can claim a witch in his family simply because hot temper shows. The flashing eyes were only a small sign. There were others. One of my aunts could get more milk from a cow than any other person, no matter how competent a milker they happened to be. She had Nan's gift. Another had a flair for smelling a storm in the wind and removing her chickens to the stone house on the very eve of a gale that rose in the hills overnight and spread the chicken

24

coops across the pasture like scattered kindling. My grandfather was a weather prophet, a horse doctor and a gifted man in other ways. One of his remedies was to kill a cat and rope its opened-out carcass to the enlarged shoulder of a mare after pouring oil on the body of the cat. The particular mare recovered, although the vet had given her up. Old Nan was in it, of course. Nan was in the eye that decided on the spot to sink a well, in the voice that whispered to a sickly animal, in the hand that gave a drench to an ailing cow or the hand that turned the churn. She listened to the wind and brought the sheep off the hill before the blizzard and once she used two dozen eggs to cover the scalded body of a child and save it from awful scars.

Nan the fey, the uncanny one, was with us foretelling the breaking of the Thames embankment when grandfather visited London, confounding our neighbours when they criticised late harvest, early sowing or the buying or selling of stock. No one laughed at the evidence. Nan was real. She had worked her own magic in her time and we all knew the stories.

Picture her as the story-tellers of the family had her, walking the roads in the locality of her farm wearing a great black cloak, a sinister figure given to talking to the evening shadows, the flickering bats and the owl flying soundlessly among the gnarled trees. Nan saw the way of the toad and the slow-worm; she knew the heron and the cures that could be made from the slime of the pike. She could compile medicine or potion from the berries of the hedge and she had no fear of the adder. When disaster happened a long way off Nan knew about it before the pedlar brought word or victory or defeat was proclaimed at the head of the town.

Once she passed a man whose nag was bogged in a peat hole and she offered to help him save his beast but the man told her to be gone. What need had he of a woman's advice? Ah, said Nan, when the time came for his horse to come out of the bog he would remember to call on her. Late that day Nan passed the place again. The horse had sunk a foot. The black bog was about its hindquarters and only its head and shoulders were clear of the peat. Nan said nothing and the owner of the horse wrung his hands in despair. A little while before dark the man called at the door of Nan's house. Did she think she could save his horse from the bog? Nan nodded and strode to the place. The man paid her five crowns. The doomed horse struggled as Nan caught its halter. The bog sucked and bubbled, but the horse rose and came out on to solid ground.

Another day Nan encountered a farmer's wife toiling at a butter churn and asked if she might have a little butter. When she was refused she remarked that the woman would be glad to give her butter before the

25

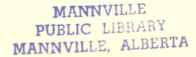

butter came. The farmer's wife churned for a day and still the cream refused to separate. Finally she sent for the witch. Nan took the handle of the churn and on one turn the buttermilk flowed and the butter was made. So many things like this she did that she became a legend. As she went for her walks country folk pointed her out to those who had not seen her before: 'The red-headed witch! Touch your cap to her in case she takes offence.' Nan was not given to taking offence and putting curses on people, by all accounts, but those who scorned her found that when their hens went off the lay they did not come back to fertility, and when their ponies went lame they remained lame. People came from round about to consult her about their husbands, wives and lovers, their fears and hopes. What Nan said would be, came to pass. What she denied was never fulfilled. When she set her face against a person they had no luck. When she smiled on them they prospered.

I am aware that this picture of Nan may be the one that those who are ashamed of her choose to tell. Perhaps she had malice in her and sat brooding before a black pot, muttering incantations and putting her blackest curses on those who offended her. The women of the family today seem to recognise old Nan's worse traits in other female relatives. It may always be so, for it takes a long long time to live down a witch and particularly such a powerful witch. Fortunately for the peace, none of the women has red hair and none is double-jointed.

Before my grandfather died I talked to him about Nan, a subject that often made him lose his temper. He was for logic. 'Nan might have been a witch, as Charles says, and she might not. She had the way of coaxing a horse and we've all had that. She had the way of making butter and your grandmother had that. She could cure an ache and make a purge. She could read the weather and she was a strong-minded body. All these things are in the kind of us. If Nan was fey, then some of us were that way before her and some have been that way since. Just let Charles have his nonsense. He thinks he has a better story than I can tell about the old folk, but Charles has his way of it and I have mine.'

I consulted my great-uncle Charles and he laughed. 'What one of the family has more of old Nan in him than your grandfather?' was what he said, 'and could you expect him to admit that he is close to a witch?'

Once I looked at a copy of the parish records and found Nan's name there. It said nothing about her double-joints and not a word about the colour of her hair, but it was enough. She was there and there is no smoke without fire. Charles was a hard-headed farmer and not really a story-teller at all. He couldn't have invented old Nan unaided, even allowing for his fine sense of humour. No, I've looked at the thing. I've examined the evidence and I'm persuaded that there is a witch in our family tree. To claim a witch and admit that she was not put to the stake detracts a little from the strength of the claim, I know, and it hardly compensates to say that the gifts of the witch were scattered among her descendants, but they were. Red-headed, double-jointed Nan was so feared that none dared set his hand against her and she died at a great age, taking with her a cure for the locked jaw and the cancer, the secret of making ale from heather, the way of moving raging toothache to one's enemy and the way of banishing warts. The things she did are not all listed. Some of the family have gifts which are unaccountable and, as great-uncle Charles said of Nan, 'I'd rather see a smile than a scowl that had the old witch in it.'

I don't laugh at the stories myself. It is not a laughing matter. I keep an eye on my son and daughter. One day the cat's hair may stand on end and the chimney blow back smoke into the room and I'll know that we're living in the tradition. Meantime, I keep a lot to myself in spite of all I've said. I hope she'll rest in my generation.

Bees in the Blood

When I was three years old, and three feet tall, my grandfather had us to the photographer's studio, not for a three-generation photograph, but for a group of four. Great-grandfather was still alive then. He had in his day kept bees, which, now that I have colonies of my own, makes me the fourth generation of the family to keep them. This is not to say that I have the wisdom of four generations. Oddly enough, my grandfather didn't keep bees while his father had colonies. My father didn't have an apiary until his father was dead, and the same applied in my own case. We all had bees in our bonnets, you might say, but then we all kept poultry, ducks, geese, bantams and the like, and if we didn't inherit know-how we at least showed that we had similar interests in common.

I can sit thinking about my childhood and actually think I hear the drone of bees that followed the sections of honey into the porch where grandfather stored the leaky ones on saucers or plates laid along a shelf. Bees were as much a part of life then as other and much larger forms of livestock. I feared the bees as much as the different bulls we had. My grandfather faced both bulls and bees with a wonderful lack of fear, and he didn't seem to get stung quite so much as my father, whose

27

temperament was different. Father handled bees the way he handled horses, with a certain determination to show who was master. He kept out of the way when grandfather was at the business and only got himself hives when the old man had been dead for some years. His bees harvested the fields of Cheshire, where he lived before he came to North Wales. He was not troubled with the business of dealing with unextractable heather honey.

Grandfather never had an extractor. His hives were full of sections, and he could hardly harvest a section before the bees were working on the ling because the summers weren't really the long hot summers one reads about in the memoirs of old men, but a mixed lot with more rain in the west than drought; otherwise the corn would never have risen nor the roots fattened.

Honey in Cheshire could be apple, clover or lime, and my father was always as proud of his honey as if he had personally gathered every spoonful. He made mead when he had too much. He got stung rather a lot. Once he had a great battle with his strongest and most pugnacious colony and retreated before it, violently sick from the hammering they had given him. He never admitted that the stings hurt him. He swore he didn't feel them at all, and now, in my generation, I begin to understand. He was not immunised against the sting. He was simply desensitised to the 'needle's' penetration, the actual pain of the sting.

At this time I kept as clear of bees as my father had done when his father was keeping them. To be honest, I was nervous of them. Only twice did I step into the line of battle, once to take a swarm from the tree outside my house and ship it by the first train to Cheshire, and the second time to help a parson neighbour of mine to get bees out of his bedroom. Most of the work was done with an improvised smoker made from fire bellows and a cocoa tin, a fly spray and a vacuum cleaner, the bag of which I filled several times to clear casualties from the minister's bedroom carpet. I shudder to think of my ignorance and callousness now.

About this time my father moved into the house in which I am now living, shipping all his bees from Cheshire to Wales and disregarding the fact that bees that are native to a certain district never really do well moved en masse to another locality. A Welsh bee is the right one for the Welsh countryside. It has thrived there. It belongs there, and generations have handed down the characteristics of the strong native strain. I am not yet qualified to say anything about imported queens, but I am convinced of this, and my father's removal seemed to prove it, for although his honey harvest had been wonderful in Cheshire his bees never did well here. They never really settled down again. Father kept them as a dilettante instead of the keen producer of honey he had been when he lived in Cheshire.

He never made so much as a gallon of mead from his excess honey or his cappings. The reason was very simple. He never got enough honey to set up his colonies for the winter. The incomers fared very much worse than long-ago invaders who came in along the seaboard. The fields didn't yield to them. The climate, and perhaps their situation within a mile of the sea, put an end to their efficiency as working colonies. My father was never a ruthless man. He didn't let the bees die. He didn't 'requeen'. He kept them for sentimental reasons. He should, of course, have got himself some Welsh bees, which was what I did in my turn.

I think that if I had inherited the Cheshire bees my enthusiasm for them, or for bees of any kind, would have wilted in a season, but I didn't inherit them. The whole apiary faded away and died in the spring when my father died. A similar thing had happened long ago when grand-father died. No one in the dreary days following a bereavement thought of looking in at the bees. The state of the hives was remarked upon when they looked dilapidated. By that time all the colonies were dead. I gave the hives away to a beekeeper who lived on the other side of the county. He said he had rarely seen such well-designed hives. I wasn't surprised. They had been built by a man who had spent a lifetime designing and planning and building. They were palaces fit for a queen. How I wish now I had kept them.

In due time, with the blessing of the church, or to be more explicit, the help of a friend who is a minister, I set up my own apiary. All my colonies with the exception of one consist of bees of the native Welsh strain. All of them work well, but the colony of Israeli bees, like those bees from Cheshire, harks back to different weather conditions, different humidity, a warmer climate and a variety of blossom not found here. The Welsh bees have risen up against me, as they were bound to do, and having been through the fire I have no fear of them now. I know that they mark a target and others come in on the same line of attack, and I take care not to be stung if I can help it. I have had two successful seasons. I have honey in jars and mead in bottles.

I begin to think it is time I studied my father and grandfather more closely. We follow in one another's footsteps. If I haven't second sight, which my grandfather had, I could perhaps make some predictions on my own future.

Perhaps the keeping of bees is only one small part of the whole pattern of the generations.

Days in the Goldfinch Field

Fields, we used to say, were like the people who owned them. In a way I suppose this is still true. Criticism of a man's fields often arose over the way he let the weeds grow, for weeds often seeded before the lazy man cut them down, and wind-borne seed sailed off to make work for his neighbours.

The goldfinch field was poorly tended. It was a reflection of the way of life pursued by the family who owned the place. They were happy-go-lucky people, more concerned with hunting the gorse bushes with a dog than doing work of any sort. They had enough stalls for forty milking cows, but they milked fewer than twenty. This meant that they brought in less hay, planted fewer fields, grew fewer turnips and let the weeds grow. It was a pleasant place, however, and on a sunny summer's afternoon when other people were busy turning hay, the little steading on the hill would be drowsy with the cooing of pigeons in the adjoining wood, the buzzing of bees that gathered honey on the unkempt fields, and the occasional crowing of a cock.

The goldfinch field was some distance away from the steading. It flanked the burn, which for most of its course ran alongside the road, but the field itself was obscured from view for a good part of its length by willows and thorns. Only here and there, where there was a gap,

30

could a passer-by see just how the wilderness grew; and grow it did, flourishing in summer like the green bay tree.

I loved to pass along the road and pause at some of the gaps in the thorns and look out across the field, especially in late summer when everything was in bloom. The burn grew such things as meadowsweet and kingcups in its silted parts. No one bothered very much about using the ditching tools, any more than they went out into the field to cut the weeds, so that one could admire the golden stars of the squalid ragwort, the brown hardheads, the cornflowers. I have always had a soft spot for the natural flowers of the wilderness. I love the delicate mauve of the hardhead, and to me thistles and teazles are handsome things even if the thorns were a curse that made anyone working in the harvest field keep a needle somewhere at hand.

The goldfinch field had several kinds of weeds, spear milk, Scotch thistles and teazles. I seem to remember that there were also creeping thistles, but those who recited the list named four out of disgust for the lazy family who let them grow. It was because of the thistles and teazles that the place was called the goldfinch field: uncut thistles tarnish a little in autumn, and when their leaves begin to die the seedheads open and the downy parachutes carrying the seed spread the plant wherever the breeze will carry them.

The goldfinches gathered in that place like swallows gathering for the journey south. What a wonderful, almost ethereal, sound was the tinkling music of scores of goldfinches. A man who has never seen goldfinches on teazles has missed something of great beauty, for there is hardly a more handsome bird.

The owners of the field were fond of birds, among other things. I remember once going up to call upon them for something my grandfather wanted. They had two cages hanging on nails on the whitewashed wall of the farmhouse. One contained a variegated canary that sang 'fit to burst', it was so happy, and the other a goldfinch caught, without a shadow of doubt, down among the thistles along the burnside. It was sad to see the wild bird there. Even I could tell it hadn't been long in its prison, for, like all newly taken wild birds, it persisted in flying upwards and colliding with the wire forming the roof of its cage. In those days a lot of wild birds were taken, especially in remote places.

There was no intentional cruelty, I think, but a lack of understanding of the happiness of a wild bird and its corresponding frenzy when confined to a cage.

The goldfinch field would have been a bird-catcher's paradise while the birds were in the locality, but they didn't stay after the teazles and

31

other weeds had seeded. All at once, when the harvest fields began to have that brown look that comes as the stubbles age, the goldfinches would be gone. This desertion of a place in which they had fed for several weeks was significant to anyone who watched the changing face of the countryside. Even the burn seemed to have a more sullen flow.

The hawthorn leaves reddened and crumbled. The blackberries, soggy and wormed, fell into the water and stained it, while out in the field the spear thistles changed into bare stalks and the docks rusted.

Such places are infrequently encountered now, I think. The weeds are cut by tractor-drawn machines, the ditches cleaned by mechanical ditching tools. The sort of people who would put off cutting weeds to ferret rabbits would go to the wall. With the weeds all cut or sprayed one doesn't expect to find a goldfinch field or hear the tinkling music of flocks of them sweeping in round the giant thistles.

Goldfinch flocks seem smaller to me these days. When I was a boy thistles and teazles were not only commoner but much taller, and so were the thorn trees and the birds that perched on them.

A Wood that Died

So many of the fine woods I knew as a boy have gone without trace that I am often quite depressed just to think of them: hog-back woods that stood on hills around the countryside, thick-clustering deciduous trees flanking quiet, deserted stretches of road, cathedral-like woods of beech, and all of them gone, exploited in the timber market.

A wood we called the low planting was probably the first I ever knew. It was certainly my first love. It grew in a hollow. Its atmosphere was moist, scented, intoxicating to a child. Because it was a planting of pine, fir, larch, and occasional birch, with only a few tough oaks and ashes seeded wild in its heart, it was almost certain to die or be cut down in my lifetime. A child doesn't think of tomorrow, however, or of the generation that planted a wood. The trees of the low planting were long past maturity when I first knew it. The thorn hedge above the ditch running along two of its sides was gnarled and ancient and seemed impenetrable. On the other two sides, a moss-capped, ferny dry-stone wall sheltered its northern and western flanks. Within hedge and walls tall pines shaded patches of bracken that grew in the welcome cover provided. A little further in larches stood on parade, straight and close-ranked as though they had taken their places at the command of a drill sergeant. Beneath them stretched a carpet of brown needles across which only the smaller creatures of the wood could pass along tunnels formed by trunks and branches.

On the northern side of the low planting a stretch of moorland ended in a boggy corner. Peaty water that gathered there welled up again inside the planting, giving life to a profusion of marsh plants that were crowded by ferns, and making a treacherous place for anyone to walk upon. I remember when I first gathered my courage and ventured over into the secret place. Disaster overtook me within a few yards. I came out again with a black stocking of wet peat. I had almost left my boots behind. They squelched water at every step I took, and they knew at home that I had been over the wall. I was warned that cattle had been known to come to grief in that place. In order to keep out intruders a long strand of rusty barbed wire hung from larch poles leaning on the inner side of the wall, but this didn't deter me from going in again. I had found nests in cavities in the wall. I was lured deeper to find a woodcock's eggs at the bottom of one of the pine trees.

The low planting had a mound at its easterly corner, a sizeable hillock that hummed with life in summer. Honey bees lived in a dead tree there. Rainflies, greenbottles and bluebottles would emerge from the fern as one struggled through them. Sometimes the air was rank with the odour of the stinkhorn, and funguses of many other kinds grew in the grass or among the pine needles. The prevailing scent was of pine and fir, the scent of resin bleeding from a damaged branch, oozing from the base of a pine or congealing on a stump fractured by the gale. Sticky resin from pine cones picked from the floor turned one's fingers black as one touched a dead stick or put a hand to the ground. I suppose I sometimes gave the family cause for anxiety by my long absences, for time and again I would watch the red squirrels throwing themselves from tree to tree. Once I stroked a hen pheasant sitting on her clutch of eggs, and there was a day when an adder and I confronted each other on a sunny bank.

What a place the wood was on a warm summer's evening when scents were even heavier and pigeons cooed or rose to clap wings and sail back down into the conifer tops. At nightfall bats were along the pasture side, flickering about under the branches that overhung the thorn hedge. Rabbits bobbed in the fields, and on the moorland side a nightjar sailed to catch moths. I loved the blanket of silence that settled on the planting when day had finally gone. I had no fear of the place, even at night when the world was eerie with the lowing of cattle and the barking of faraway dogs. When I was ten years old I knew the wood so well I could have walked through it blindfolded, locating the ditch by the sound of water trickling into it from hill drains, and the moor by the hushing of wind in tall, straggling gorse bushes a little way out from the wall. Summer or winter, the planting was snug, a sheltering place, a roost for the pheasant, perch for the long-eared owl, the kingdom of stoats living in a stone pile on the mound. Carrion crows called at twilight. Cock pheasants flapped their wings and challenged each other on spring mornings.

I was forbidden to take a gun into the low planting when the time came for me to be given a gun. The estate keeper didn't put birds down there, but he fed the ground from time to time. Pheasants that took shelter could be driven out on a shooting day. It wasn't only the keeper's preserve, however, for the country blacksmith would go there once in a while and snare pheasants, using a device I had better not describe in detail. I suppose that if the keeper didn't detect the blacksmith's visit he knew my footprints, for he came to complain that I had released a cat from one of his traps. He may have regarded the planting as his domain, but it was mine too. I cut my first fishing rod there. I sat in the top of a larch tree once, reading fragments of a newspaper I found in a rook's nest. There was a rookery in the very heart of the larches. One frosty autumn day I actually made a fire in the planting, roasting newly-dug potatoes in its embers and improving the feast with salty farm butter and a bottle of buttermilk.

It was a kind of fairytale place to me, even as I grew into my teens; but the magic was tarnishing a little. Someone cut a few larches to make fence posts or rick props for the stackyard (a well-built rick never needed propping) and the damage was done. Maintenance work of this and other kinds resulted in gaps in the larches. The axe had felled a few trees. The gales felled more. The woodcock went away, and the rooks too, in the end. Somehow wintering bullocks won their way to the blanket of the ferns and the shelter of tall larches. They had barged their way through the brittle and crumbling barrier of thorns, breaking the bank of the ditch.

I was saddened by all this when I went to the low planting after a long absence. It wasn't just that cobwebs hung in the high branches of those tottering larches. The few deciduous trees were diseased. Every winter the pines suffered the heavy loads of winter snow with less resilience. At last someone gave the order to grub out the broken hedge, clear out the weedy ditch, haul away the fallen trees and fell the remainder. I didn't see the death of the wood. I never saw the tidied-up site, for the family

34

had gone by then. I never had the heart to go again to visit such a happy childhood scene.

Last summer, however, I was given an aerial photograph of the locality, a colour picture. The bareness and desolation of it all made me sigh. All woods die in time, of course, and I am no longer a child. Trees are no more immortal than man is. Immortality is in the minds of those who live to remember. I remember the warbling of the wren in that wood, and the cooing of the pigeons 50 years ago.

Pine Martens in Secret Places

Perhaps the excitement that the sight of a rare bird such as the kite sometimes generates is more widespread because ornithologists and bird-watchers have a chance, albeit a somewhat remote one, of seeing migrants and wandering birds from time to time. Talk of a very rare creature such as the pine marten, which is found in the forest not so many miles from my home (as the raven flies), promotes discussion, but the excitement is almost momentary and the interest shown in the first place flags and dies when one is compelled to decline to give the locality. A pine marten becomes a sort of abominable snowman, a Loch Ness monster. The average man has to be 'shown' and when the story can only be repeated as something 'on good authority', an account of pine martens in the forest is not nearly as romantic as talk of wolves and beavers in the days when Geraldus was touring Wales. The wolf, the beaver and the eagle belong in legend here. There is a beaver pool on the river. Snowdon is the proper place of eagles. The wolves probably gave up in Wales before they were killed off, for the pickings were indeed thin.

Who gives thought to the fact that the pine marten managed to hang on in the wilds of Wales and survived, like the polecat, while almost everywhere else it was near to extinction? The trouble is that there are so few pine martens (unlike our polecats which have multiplied and flourished in the past ten years until they are the bane of most keepers' lives) that practically no one sees them, and the few people who do have a glimpse of them keep quiet about it. There is a price on every rare and almost extinct creature. I heard a hundred pounds mentioned as the sum awaiting the person who would deliver up the pine martens. It is highly unlikely that the reward will be claimed, even if it is doubled or trebled, but no one is taking any chances.

The polecat's wandering ways are notorious, and its casual resemblance to the altogether more handsome pine marten lead to people hurrying to have their 'pine martens' verified by someone who knows them if they happen to see something on the fringe of the forest. All cats are grey and all slinky, brown, ferret-like creatures are martens to the person who indulges in wishful thinking. The truth is that the marten shares some of the less attractive habits of the polecat. It will come down and hunt for the eggs of gamebirds. It is, after all, a member of the *Mustelidae* family and a hunter, taking mice, rats and rabbits. Its tail is bushier, its legs are longer, its head broader, and its colouring much more attractive than that of the sombre polecat; for its bright yellow or creamy throat and frontal shoulder markings are most distinctive. Above all, despite its family, the marten lacks the nauseous odour of the polecat. When it runs through the trees searching for the nest of a bird, or some almost helpless fledgling it may find at roost, it has a less sinister appearance than the polecat, which always seems to ripple over rough terrain as though its short legs were a serious handicap. The fact is, of course, that a polecat is more effectively designed for hunting under fallen trees, through holes in walls and the boles of trees than for the more open world of the high trees in which the marten travels.

The marten is on the ground a great deal, of course, not only because a great amount of food stubbornly refuses to come up into the treetops. Young grouse on the fringe of the forest are less likely to perch on a tree than on a high wall, and voles, mice and many small birds are similarly unaccommodating in their habits. It isn't only for the mammals that the pine marten descends to ground level, however. In due season it proves itself less blood-thirsty than its relatives, the polecats, stoats and weasels, for it takes a little fruit for dessert, the bilberry that grows on the peat banks, and sometimes the wild raspberry growing in the shelter of the lichened forest wall.

It is said that the marten was at one time something of a menace to the fruit in the garden of the hill farmer or the shepherd, and would raid the beehives. The location of our resident martens suggests that it is unlikely that they ever get a taste of honey. I expect that they have a late summer feast of bilberries and crowberries, and maybe blackberries here and there. For the most part their diet will be upland birds, young grouse, perhaps, if they find them in the heather; pipits and long-tailed tits, if they can beard the gorse bush; a great feast of wood mice and voles; and occasionally perhaps, a leveret. That they are breeding has already been established, and that they wander is known, although confirmation of their wanderings is rarely offered by those who know that they move out of their breeding area.

A friend who was fishing one of the remote hill lakes one day got his fly fast in a spruce tree and found himself looking up at a very handsome rich brown creature a little over two feet in length and with the characteristic markings of the marten. He came to tell me about it before he mentioned it to anyone else, and I persuaded him to call his marten a large tree-climbing polecat, which he did when I assured him that he was getting a little 'warm'.

If the marten is to hold its own and multiply, the secret must be kept.

The Road Across the Moss

Nostalgia is a complaint that springs from a state of mind. It can hardly be cultivated, for I have tried. A couple of summers ago I went back to enjoy a sentimental journey and travel across the moss by a route I often travelled in my boyhood. The skyline was unchanged. I recognised the ancient landmarks, the lichened dikes, the bilberry hillocks, peat ruts where the old peat cuttings had fallen in, and the prominent boulders and rocky mounds that were milestones on the way, long ago when I was young and innocent.

The trouble was the the road was shorter, smoother and more straight than it once was, and wider by half a cart at least. There were no rabbits hopping on the green that marked either side of the strip that horses once walked, hauling carts of peat or hay, or milk churns back from the creamery. There were no grouse picking grit, piled where the cartwheels scattered it and the moorland rainstorms washed it. Some of the finest heather had gone and where it had once flourished there was green, coarse grass that even the black-faced sheep couldn't browse upon. Gone was the lyre-tailed black cock from the fir planting's edge and the smell of burning peat from the hidden-away lodge in the trees.

I thought about the futility of going back to anything, for nothing remains the same, but I should have walked. Had I done so I might have had a breath of the moss, enjoyed the scents of the wilderness and, in my slow journey between my old landmarks, conjured up a vision of the peat-cutters of my childhood, the shepherd out on the distant slope with his gathered flock bumping along between his two best dogs, and the sound of his whistle coming faintly across that breeding ground of curlew and grouse, nightjar and owl, woodcock and snipe.

Long ago we 'camped' there in the bright summer sun, drinking smoky tea, eating food we had brought in a big pan basket before barrowing peats along well-defined paths to the light carts on which they were finally transported home to keep our winter fires burning. Out there, too, were the old butts used by shooting parties that now had no grouse to shoot on the twelfth, and the cairns put up in memory of some shepherd whose soul would haunt the place forever.

We used to cross the moss to go to Alticry where we had our shore picnics. Every yard of the way was significant and full of minor wonders then, like an adder's corpse, flattened again and again by the wheels of carts and gigs, and a fierce cat that glared at us from the shelter of the trees and might just, with a slight stretch of the imagination, have been descended from the true wildcat my father encountered when he climbed the shore crags, barefooted and sunburned on his school holidays. At one place the burns ran one way and a few yards on went down another watershed entirely. Here we were that much closer to the sea and able to watch, as the gig went slowly downhill, the watercourse enlarging and water cascading into better and better falls.

For a long time I thought this was the Grey Mare's Tail my elders talked about when we were in that part of the world, but I was disappointed to discover that the Grey Mare's Tail wasn't a cascade of water but a strip of grey road that dropped to the sea like the mare's tail. Before the sight of the sea there were the cothouses, those little, huddling stone cottages in which farm labourers lived and their children swarmed in well-cultivated gardens. They all stopped whatever they were doing to see us pass and stared without shame, their eyes large and their mouths open, and we never exchanged a word for we were all too shy. We trundled through their world and, when we were well past, we would hear them laughing and talking as before, the young ones shrilling, excited dogs barking. Nostalgia from the four-wheel soft suspension of a modern motor car? It is almost impossible to create such a thing.

I didn't have time to walk the moorland road and indulge the dream as it should have been indulged, or step off the hard road to wade the heather or breast the bracken and find the spring where the burn had its source. Here the first of a hundred little green and yellow trout had a private domain in a miniature pool shaded by ferns.

Once, of course, this was the whole world, or almost all of it between me and the blue hills of the far horizon. Once I knew exactly where the waterhen nested and the first really deep pool in the burn's course, where, just after the spate, a really big trout would gulp down the worm and dive for the shelter of an outsized boulder. Once I knew the stare of the tousle-headed Highland cattle the owner of that part of the moss kept to please his fancy, and the sad and lonely donkey that walked on up-turned hooves because the land was too soft to keep his nails pared.

The stuff of dreams needs to be cultivated and nurtured, fed, once in a while, with a little reality that is, with every passing year, harder and harder to find, but sweeter than anything when it is discovered because it promotes wonderful remembrance.

Idols of my Childhood

Every boy has his idols, and there would be something wrong if he didn't find a certain fascination in the men of his time. Mine, I confess, weren't very high idols, although they improved a shade as time went on. The first of them were characters of the town, and I watched them, round-eyed and awed, from the well of a gig while my elders transacted business in the ironmonger's or some such emporium. The women of the family greatly deplored my admiration for a one-armed poacher, who smoked a blackened clay pipe, and my preoccupation with an assortment of 'weather men' who stood on the flags at the corner of the square, withdrawing to shelter when it rained and coming out to enjoy the sun when shadows of clouds went scudding away across distant hills. They felt that a small boy should be given some standard of fit conduct.

The idlers of the town might be colourful and romantic, especially when they went off goose or duck shooting with their ancient guns, but they were idlers. They were drunkards; good-for-nothing, tobacco-chewing scoundrels; and they were mostly unwashed. This didn't make them any less fascinating, so far as I was concerned, for I couldn't even pass a tinker's brood or a shuffling tramp without staring. If a gipsy or a travelling fiddler (the very last of these, and what were called ballad singers, were still upon the roads) called at the door, I was there to study them, to walk away with them, in imagination, with my whippet at my heel and my blackened tea-can swinging from my hand.

This was no way for a child to regard the world, of course. If some of my elders chose to exchange the time of day with town characters or vagrants walking from nowhere to nowhere, that was all very well. They had already made their assessment of the important things of life. A boy needed to be taught respect for honest toil, for craftsmanship and all the things that made it possible for the minority of vagrants, poachers and ne'er-do-wells to loiter, poach and spit between their boots. It soon became a rule that when a horse wanted shoes, or a ploughsock repointing, I was sent to the smithy. When a repair was done to a flail or a bindersheet needed new slats, I went to the joiner's with whoever took it. When corn had to be milled, I went to the miller's. I was encouraged to watch old Jock, the best thatcher for miles, and to see how Tam rebuilt a length of wall. I was even encouraged to carry traps for the

40

one-legged mole-catcher (the mowdie man) and never missed an outing with him when he was making one of his periodic visits.

All this, of course, was in the interests of my forming an appreciation of a man's worth. The smith might be a bit rough-tongued, but when he worked he worked until his swarthy face became streaked with perspiration that ran from his eyebrows. He wrought wonders in iron from a volcano of coal or peat. I used to hold horses for him when horses still towered above me as mammoths might have done. More than once I quenched hot iron in a tank, and I worked the bellows handle from a perch on top of a suitable box, although this was only when the task involved none of the critical heats required for hand-welding iron.

The joiner wore a suit of rusty overalls, and his equipment included a donkey engine that coughed and panted and drove a saw. Here the atmosphere was one of yellow pine, dusty beech and sour-smelling oak. Sometimes the air was scented with resin or strong with the clean smell of red-lead paint. Outside the shop half-a-dozen blue, red or green-painted carts pointed their shafts to the sky, and twice as many wheels lay against the wall waiting to be shod with rims of iron, heated and then shrunk in place with water poured from a can. Here I watched the building of stairs for a loft, the making of meal arks, and cradles for babies unborn. The smith might be my chief idol, but the joiner had second place, because he made a wheel-barrow or a butter churn with equal ease and I liked the smell of fresh shavings better than burning hoof.

The miller, on the other hand, controlled a machine of great power. It rumbled and rattled and the old stone building was filled with the sound of something like a minor thunderstorm before we traded our sacks of oats for milled wheat and oatmeal. There was the millrace, too, and the water that fed it at the lifting of a gate. The peaty flood set the wheel turning and the shafting groaning. There were trout in the water, too. I used to see them when the sun shone on the yellowish water, anchored behind boulders, out of the full force of the current. The miller was a watcher of trout. Beneath his coat of white dust he was a burly fellow with a fine tan, but no one would have thought so.

A fair selection of minor idols followed these main ones. There was a horse-breaker who came once a year to train to chains, or shafts, one of the young horses my grandfather had bred. What fearless, bold fellows horse-breakers were, so very different from horse-dealers, in whose company no child might be left for fear he might pick up language no respectable child should ever hear. As a town boy wants to drive a railway engine, I wanted to break horses; but then, I also wanted to

41

thatch a row of tall ricks and crown them with that final dolly decoration from the top of the very longest ladder in the place (I have never had any sort of head for heights, so it is perhaps just as well that this ambition faded).

Old Frank was another sort of idol. He doctored pigs and calves with an incredibly sharp pocket-knife, but it was for his skill with a gun that I admired him. He could lure stoats from a stone-heap by blowing on a blade of grass placed between his lips, and shoot two before they had a chance to skip back to cover.

Good solid men built dry-stone walls, march walls to stand forever and intermediate walls to stand almost as long. I used to watch them when we had walling done as well as when I went to shows, and saw them competing with each other as shoe-smiths did. The mole-catcher limped about the lower fields and woodsides, setting his traps and garnering his harvest of skins. I was a great admirer of his, although it was said that he was but half a step from being a poacher and a rogue himself. In the town I watched the harness-maker pad and fit a cart-horse's collar. I stood for hours to see coopers mending barrels. Even the working tinker, when he came to mend a pot, was an example to me for he, too, ate bread by the sweat of his brow and was a sort of country craftsman. Once I spent a whole morning at a clog-maker's, for most dairymen and stockmen wore brass-bound clogs. I came away with thoughts of working with sharp knives and shaping tools, making clogs for everybody in the country.

Most of all, however, I used to picture myself as a blacksmith with a stream by my door, with bantams dust-bathing at the bottom of my garden hedge, with an anvil to ring, with trout to catch and mornings to fish the black dam. None of this was to be. My unromantic schoolmasters saw to that. I suppose my father had visions of a similar sort in his day, and my grandfather, too, had his rural idols who faded or departed and were forgotten.

Three or four years ago, remembering some of my fond dreams while visiting scenes of my childhood, I went past the smithy. No bantams fed on a midden, and no horses stood tethered at the ring waiting to be shod, but a blue flash behind the half-obscured window told the story of an arc welder at work; and then a man who was no smith poked his head out of the door as he pushed goggles on to his brow. The mill, when I passed it, was silent and blind, its doors and windows boarded. The joiner had no rank of carts on the grassy knoll by his door, and the panting engine breathed no more. It is true that in a village I saw a one-legged man who might have been my mole-catcher blessed with eternal youth, but where were the old thatcher, the cooper, the clog-maker, the horse-breaker and those tireless dry-stone wallers? Their ghosts may have been somewhere about the countryside, just as the ghosts of the loungers may have been propping corners of the town square, but I didn't see them, and I was sorry to have looked and found them missing.

Tinkers on the Road

The last tinkers I saw in Galloway were a small family of five who rode upon the old-time tinker's barrow and waited at the end of the village street while the father of the tribe played bagpipes and begged from door to door. This was about 15 years ago, and I marked them for tinkers because of the way they lived, cadging. They had the same hard look of the tinkers of my childhood. They lived by their wits. A time had been when they would have had a jangle of cans of different sorts dangling from the tailboard of their barrow and advertising their coming, and the man with the bagpipes would have had some skill at tinning a kettle or a teapot or soldering a hole beneath its spout.

My childhood impression of tinkers was of little convoys of them on their way about the quiet roads of an even quieter countryside. Even in those days they were coming to the end of the line. All kinds of modern innovations were making the tin kettle and the old-fashioned impedimenta of the kitchen obsolete. Countrywomen were cooking over paraffin stoves and more sophisticated ranges. People were throwing away copper kettles. Tinkers were soliciting work, and when there was none, hiring themselves as casual labour, although farmers were wary of casuals who looked as though labour might come amiss to them. The native tinker was redundant, forced to become a cadger. His son no longer pretended to be able to mend a pot.

There was a time in midsummer when even the tinkers were welcome if they could be persuaded to 'wage' at turnip thinning or 'back weeding', which was a hands-and-knees business of crawling the rows pulling the prolific growth of chickweed, groundsel and charlock. Farmers who took a family on were careful to see that they nailed down things otherwise easily removed. They counselled their wives to make diligent search for the eggs of lay-away hens. They looked the field for snares. They counted their ducks, and into the bargain made sure that there was no smoking in the barn or outhouse in which tinkers slept. When they left there was sure to be something missing—a setting of eggs, a bit of harness, a hank of rope, a length of plough chain. It was part of the price paid in emergency.

The tinkers were not gypsies but they were travelling families our grandfathers and great-grandfathers had known. They had names like Kyle or Irving. They came from Ireland or some other little-known place. They had been coming since time immemorial. They were like the migrating geese. People who travelled reported seeing them far away on some lonely road in Ayrshire, picking potatoes in a field near the shore perhaps, or camped in a thorn thicket with their barrows on the verge and their ponies wandering. No one ever knew what prompted them to go in one direction and not another, or what came over them when they drifted away. The few that still carried on the trade despised those who could not solder a pot and were reduced to thievery or begging. I can remember my grandmother having a teapot tinned just to please an aged tinker who had not been able to persuade anyone to let him practise his skills for a long time. It was a wonderful job of heating the teapot to a point where the solder of the spout might have melted but did not. When the pot, which had been scoured and treated to remove all grease, was at exactly the right heat it was rocked in the tinker's hands, the tin washed on and wiped off to perfection so that the pot was at once as good as new again.

Even in my childhood the tinkers were tending to integrate with the local people here and there. Like all incomers, their admission was noted. It was remembered that they came of tinker stock, and if they ever fell from grace the subject would be brought up. 'Ah, but' some old farmer would remind his audience, 'you've forgotten that his old mother was a tinker!' Tinker implied not a man who had simply become redundant at his trade, a trade still called for in the cities and industrial areas, but a horse trader, picker-up of things that did not belong to him, a sly fellow, a hard drinker, a lier-behind-the-hedge. 'Count your fingers after you shake hands with the likes of him,' they would say, 'for you're bound to find some missing.' It preserved the image of a shiftless incomer.

There are no tinkers left now for the simple reason that there is no tinkering to be done. The pace of life has overtaken them. They have gone along the undulating road into the blue distance, laughing, quarrelling, singing, fighting, taking all they could carry with them. I looked back at them with a certain fascination tinged with fear. They were hard. They were cunning. They knew how to survive. I like to think that they changed their ways. That they finally gave up being degenerate tinkers, turned to cadgers and got away, rolled along the road at the same pace as the rest of us, and changed their names from the tribal ones.

Once in a while here in Wales I come upon a sort of rally of trucks and motor caravans parked on the roadside and surrounded by people who are not gypsies but just could be the descendants of the tinkers of long ago. The only place I have seen the same faces is in the west of Ireland, where tinkers are still to be found, although it puzzles me to know what they find to solder and tin.

The Passing of the Ballad Singer

When I was a child there were still a few itinerant fiddlers, storytellers and ballad singers on the road. They were few and far between of course, and because of this their arrival at the door of the somewhat remote farm in which my grandparents lived was something that caused a stir. These travelling characters were not always too well-dressed and deodorants hadn't been developed.

Grandfather, however, loved to hear old songs sung, old tunes scraped out on the fiddle, tales told by men who made their living by telling the tale. The ballad singer was becoming extinct, as the corncrake would in due time vanish from a countryside in which it was no longer able to find a welcome. Between whiles we were a self-entertaining people. Everyone played an instrument, recited, sang or told the tale, no matter how shy or reticent they might be. Grandfather would recite, read prose in the fine style that Winston Churchill came to acquire, a sort of biblical emphasis on words that was most impressive; or when he wasn't reading, reciting or telling stories, get up and take a whirl in an eightsome reel. It was that kind of world.

Neighbours came and sang at the piano. There were some fine voices, albeit untrained ones. I sang *Tom Bowling* myself, in a quavering voice, and blushed to the applause. I was never very enthusiastic about Sunday hymns in the parlour, played by an aunt who once had her dress ruined by a candle that collapsed, pouring hot wax down the fretted front of her instrument, across the keys and into her lap before she could get clear of the piano stool. The change must have come when the phonograph came. It wasn't exactly evident to me in my generation. The phonograph had been consigned to the woodwormed shelves of the old cheese loft by then, and I never heard it play. Its place was taken by a louvre-fronted gramophone that gave us *If You Were the Only Girl in the World*, which the women milkers sang for days on end.

I didn't know that this was really the start of the rot, the end of the Victorian era of home entertainment, the use of imagination and natural talent. My father didn't know it either. He was a wireless enthusiast. Being of a technical mind, he played with crystal sets, and 'tube' wireless sets, even before 2LO. He came once, hot-foot from Glasgow, to bring the sound of music to the peaceful parlour in Galloway, bringing all kinds of things with him, from coils of cotton-covered wire and bottles of shellac to soldering irons and spirits of salts. We were to be the first in the entire kingdom of Galloway to hear voices, and even music, behind the static, the crackle and egg-frying that earphones or horn-speaker couldn't eliminate. A prophet is not without honour save in his own land. The Galloway hills, and the low power of the sending station perhaps, prevented the miracle.

Father returned to the city and his engineering a little cast down. It was a long time before the problems were solved and first wireless, and finally television, put paid to my musical aunt singing *The Wild Colonial Boy* or some red-faced, well-scrubbed ploughman rendering *The Londonderry Air* or *My Grannie's Highland Home* to an enraptured audience. The trouble with any generation is that it rarely realises change is taking place. Only in retrospect does it see that another generation had a gift. Necessity was the mother of invention, the very patron of genius, the fertiliser of talent, to say the least.

46

The ballad singers departed. The old fiddlers who were still about begged more often than they played. The story-tellers were hard put to find an audience, and when they did it was almost invariably composed of the older generation that had appreciated homespun stories and often-repeated legends. The critics of the story were dying out. Once it hadn't mattered that the story wasn't new. What counted was the slight variation in the telling, the touch of artistry. Singing and playing had been judged in a similar way. Cousin James could sing a sentimental ballad better than anyone for 50 miles. No one could make the mothed piano reverberate or sound so good as Mary Ellen or Ellen Jane. The gramophone gave us only one rendering of the songs the recording stars of the day chose to sing. The radio spoke tonelessly to us, and there was no exchange between us and it.

We should have known what was happening. The musical evening was over. No one would pick up the violin and learn to play it. Strathspeys to the gramophone would never have the same abandon as a dance to the fiddle with the lamps going red in the sudden draught.

I thought about this the other day when a friend asked me to come and examine an old phonograph, the device that, I suppose, together with that horrible instrument that came from America, the pianola, tolled the knell of honest, simple pleasure. It was a phonograph in extraordinary fine condition, a collector's piece. With it, protected from the ravages of mildew and damp, were a set of reels or spools. These had been housed in an old hatbox and emerged to be played again and conjure up memories of long ago.

There were 20 of them and the titles give some indication of the catholic taste of the Anglesey farming family whose treasured acquisition that long-horned phonograph must have been. The Welsh people were surely the last to allow canned entertainment to take over. They love the natural voice. They love poetry, story-telling and the like. Here, however, in the depth of the plain of the island, someone felt the need of something more sophisticated. It was the thin edge of the gramophone, beginning with *Ton y Botel (Tune of the Bottle)* and *Aberystwyth* by the Welsh Choir, and *My Old Man,* recorded, with orchestral accompaniment, by Tom Owen. Harry Dearth recorded *Will O' the Wisp,* Edward Davies *Y Gwenith Gwyn (The Ripe Wheat); Tra La La* was the work of Ben Albert. David Brazell recorded *Bradwraith y Don, Merch y Cadben, Cymru fy Ngwlad, Yr Eneth Ddall,* freely translated as *The Treacherous Sea, The Captain's Daughter, Wales my Country,* and *The Blind Girl.* These were the product of Sterling Records and the Russell Hunting Record Company of London.

47

Something lighter were the records from Edison Bell costing a shilling, and earnestly requested to be played at precisely 160 rpm. They were Harry Lauder's *Stop Yer Ticklin', Jock;* Florrie Ford's *There's Always Room for a Girl; Three Jolly Scotchmen,* by Jack Lorimer; *Where, oh Where,* by Billy Williams; *Mr John Mackie,* by D. McKechnie; *John, Go and Put your Trousers on,* by H. Grant; and *Punch and Judy,* a descriptive piece that was a straightforward recording of a Punch and Judy show. There was also the *Overture Raymond,* by the Royal Military Band, and *All for Jesus,* recorded by W. McEwan. *The Irish Maid* was recorded by the International Phonograph and Indestructible Record Company (Petit's Patents).

I always feel that a man's choice of music tells a great deal about him. Inquiry of the old lady who had owned the phonograph, inheriting it from her grandparents, revealed an amusing story. Grandmother had quite obviously chosen the Welsh and religious recordings. Grandfather had plumped for Harry Lauder and the Jolly Scotchmen. The more staid music had been tolerated indoors, but poor old grandfather had had to resort to subterfuge to hear his favourite pieces. The old lady recalled that grandmother had regarded Harry Lauder as some kind of depraved, drunken singer. In order to enjoy *Stop Yer Ticklin', Jock* grandfather would steal out to the gorse bushes on a hillock near the farm, and there, suspending the horn of the instrument from a stick pushed into the ground, he enjoyed himself in his own depraved way.

Neither husband nor wife could have dreamed what a pass things would come to, as they too contributed to the banishment of the fiddler and the ballad-singer.

The Decline of the Blacksmith

Some people who have taken an interest in the ancient crafts of the country might claim that, while the thatcher's and wheelwright's trades have declined, the country blacksmith has undergone a metamorphosis to emerge as a super-mechanic or a sort of agricultural engineer. There may be outward indications that this is so, but it seems to me that in this generation the blacksmith who was a craftsman has been made superfluous. The main need for the old blacksmith's particular skills has gone; indeed his very individuality in the working of metals would hardly be encouraged by implement manufacturers whose trade and business

48

depend to a great extent on parts lists, standardisation, and fixed limits laid down by a design office.

The old smith fashioned his implements to satisfy a sort of instinct for the operation with which they were concerned. He judged the set of a plough by his eye and the balance of the thing when he held the stilts in his hands. He forged iron to take a shape that his father, grandfather or great-grandfather had predetermined, for his was craftsmanship to which generations had contributed. There was no drawing, except perhaps with a piece of chalk or the point of a nail scratching on the iron hood of the hearth. Rarely were the products of the smithy exactly identical, because repetition is not in the nature of the craftsman.

There was a time when the corncrake was heard in almost every meadow as summer was advancing. They say that the mechanical reaper was responsible for the corncrake's being banished, for it was the first of the mechanical monsters and a humble ancestor of the combine. Perhaps the corncake perished in the hayfield as its eggs were crushed, its young destroyed. To the smith who had struggled to feed his family by making ploughs, harrows, iron gates and iron hoops for cartwheels, the mechanical reaper must have seemed a blessing. The man who could understand mechanisms and repair a machine that hadn't as yet any sort of production line behind it, and few spare parts that could be easily obtained, found that he could make a better living and still work at his craft without smothering his creative ability entirely. Every mechanical reaper had to be drawn by horses, as indeed had the binder that followed it into the harvest field, and there was hope that if harvesting became more economical farming might prosper.

In days gone by, the more fortunate smiths had patrons—landowners on whom they depended for their tenancies and to whom they could go for work to enable them to pay their rent, but with the advent of the reaper and binder there was more work in some places than could be comfortably managed. The need for smiths often resulted in journeymen —men out of their time—setting up rural forges in places where the existing smiths had too much to do. Most of these old forges are derelict now, and the craftsmen who worked in them have long since vanished, because no sooner had the designer perfected his mechanical reaper than another expert stepped in to consider the problem of rigging the steam engine or the internal-combustion engine to the tools the draught horse was working.

The smith toiled on, of course. His yard was well filled with ploughs and broken binders that still showed signs of weaknesses on different land. Before the ploughing season the smith had to take horses in strict

49

rotation, and the pile of discarded shoes sometimes equalled the midden. The bellows creaked and groaned, the volcano of the hot coals erupted, the sparks flew up, and the quenching tank steamed and rumbled as the iron cooled. The designers worked at their drawing-boards without much advertisement, except when trials were necessary, and the smith was too busy to ask what they were doing. Now and again he took an apprentice and taught him his secret way of tempering a bit of Swedish steel or setting the 'sock' of a plough. They inspected their work by the oil lamp, and the anvil sometimes rang far into the night. The smith had never been exactly prosperous, but these were his golden days if he ever had any.

How does an ancient craft cease to be significant in a generation? The factors that have contributed to the decline of the country blacksmith are urban and numerous. In a way Mr Henry Ford had a hand in it by showing what could be done in the field of intensive production of cars, for when tractors and their auxiliary equipment came at length in full flood the production line was a necessity. Tractors, unlike horses, needed no feeding when they were stabled, and this fact was emphasised by the salesman. The smith wasted no time in teaching his latest apprentice how to put shoes on a mare, and when time hung on his hands the apprentice hankered for tools his master hadn't got—the welding torch among them—and experience he might gain in the implement yards on the fringes of country towns. The smith's apprentice saw himself as a mechanic, a welder or fitter of some kind, and he found nothing attractive in tinkering with broken and worn-out tools that no forward-looking farmer would give room to.

If the smith wouldn't become urbanised, the apprentice was determined to have none of his trade. The banker had a hand in all this, too, because he found it reasonable to recommend loans to men investing in new mechanical equipment. It began to matter very little that the smith could design a handsome set of iron gates on the back of an old envelope, even if they were a work of art. The youth with the welding torch could do that job, given a few jigs and a simple blueprint. Who would waste time taking something to the smith for a running repair when at the depot a new component could be obtained? The smith might have ingenious ways of improvising and repairing things no one else would touch, but so, in harsh truth, had the itinerant tinker.

The super mechanic is not the natural descendant of the country craftsman by any stretch of imagination. He may know how to fit bearings, tap a hole, grind a bush, replace a seal, but he doesn't create. His welding torch, which he handles with great skill, is sticking-plaster first-aid for the gap in the stock of spares or the manufacturer's lack of foresight, but he doesn't belong in the old smith's world. If he did, he would be hard put to it to shoe a stallion, fashion chain-link harrows at the anvil without a drawing or a pattern, or make a single-furrow plough capable of turning the earth.

Such ancient skills are dying fast. In the past 20 years hundreds of old smiths have retired and few have handed on their skills or found anyone who wanted them, like the smith who retired in the part of the world in which I live. He claimed to have been the last smith in Britain who could shoe oxen, and he had done so in the years between the two wars. This was a sad retirement, I felt, and yet the writing was on the wall of that village blacksmith's shop when I visited it in 1940.

Today there may be bodies interested in preserving rural crafts, against the pattern of engineered production; but as far as the smith is concerned their interest can only be dilettante, their hope forlorn. The smith of old may have made all kinds of things from picklocks to ploughs, but I doubt very much whether he and the modern implement designer have much in common or would understand each other's approach. And no one can reasonably deny that a diminuendo in the ring of the hammer on the anvil is anything but the death knell of the country smith.

Catching a Train

Both catching trains and meeting trains used to be an event in our lives. The nearest railway station was a five-mile drive by pony and trap and there were two trains a day. It was a branch line. To catch a main line train—the express—meant ignoring the branch line and intercepting the express at its nearest stopping place, seven miles away. It did not wait long there. It was the Irish boat train and it either hurried south to London or it tore on west to unload its passengers at the harbour.

It came thundering through the Galloway hills, lurching and swaying across the seemingly endless moorland where the black-faced sheep sheltered in the peat hags and the grouse were occasionally flushed from a heather bank. It whistled in the hills to waken people in those white-washed cothouses in the wilderness. It was full of sound and fury and on a very calm morning it could be heard 20 miles away, down in the Machars of Wigtownshire. It had a sort of romantic wonder for me.

On many a golden morning I stood on the stubble field and listened to the train going through.

Meeting a train had the warmth of anticipation about it, a climax of greetings, an exchange of news; but catching the train was something different. We were hardly ever able to do so with time in hand. For some reason everything had to go in a frantic rush. It was always after harvest when the Irish harvesters were impatient to be back home working on their own farms.

I remember one late September morning when I almost failed to intercept the express. It stands clear in my recollections of yesterday as one of my greatest drives. The pony had always been full of fire. He would put his nose into the corn ladle and steal the oats before you could put a bridle anywhere near his ears. If you caught his forelock, he would swing you off your feet and he had a way of spinning round and kicking the ladle so that it sailed through the air like some sort of duck falling into the rushes. The thing to do, of course, was to catch the pony in good time for the train; but when he was free on a 20-acre field, and away up at the march wall at that, it was far simpler to pretend that he would be down near the home paddock at first light. He never was, and he was not on the occasion of my great drive. He took some catching that morning, but I had him harnessed and in the gig when the harvester (there was only one working a contract this particular year) came clattering down the steps with his bundle of clothes. He was afraid that we would not catch the express and he would have to travel home on the Monday, there being no train stopping on Saturday night. It was useless trying to overcome the harvester's fear of missing the train. The only thing to do was to drive so fast that he would have to hold on and keep his mouth shut.

The grandfather clock chimed as we left. I knew, and the harvester knew, that we hadn't a minute to spare. The pony was a fine trotter. He was hard in the mouth. The tighter the rein, the closer his head came to his chest, the more his neck arched, the faster his neat hooves pounded the road. There was no holding him once he took off. He set his ears, dilated his nostrils and travelled like the wind with no thought of slowing on a bend lest he tipped us into the ditch. The grit spurted from the wheels and sometimes the pony's shoes made sparks on the stones. The Irish harvester quickly forgot about the train. I forgot about it too, for although I pretended to be urging the pony to greater efforts I knew he could go no faster. He had run off. I was no more in control than was my passenger!

We went downhill and uphill at the same pace. We flashed past cothouses with their curtains drawn, we frightened cattle browsing on the hedges, we sent rabbits scampering for the shelter of their burrows, frightened crows and magpies from the wayside oaks and ash trees. My eyes streamed tears and flecks of foam flew from the pony's flanks. The train could be heard emerging from the hills, crossing the flat country on the way to our point of interception, but only just heard. The sound of our own locomotion filled the air and grew even worse when, rounding a bend with the gig lurching dangerously, we came upon an iron gate that had somehow swung outwards and half-blocked the road. The pony swerved, the hub of a wheel crashed the iron gate aside and we went even faster.

I had visions of our crashing through the white fence at the station and the harvester going home in a coffin, but at the entrance to the station the pony almost sat on his haunches. We came to a jolting halt. The harvester got down very shakily and ran like a terrified fowl to the entrance to the platform.

I should add, perhaps, that we went home a great deal more steadily. I stabled the pony, rubbed him down and kept him stabled until the afternoon. Grandfather came in to see me after his midday inspection. 'It seems you drove the pony hard this morning,' he said. 'Was there need of that?' I replied with complete honesty. There had been no need. He had had wings on his heels and we had had an angel flying above us.

Horse for Sale

When a working horse might be bought for £25 or so and ponies for £5 or even less there were two or three ways of coming by the sort of animal needed. One was to go to the market and buy a horse which stood there to be looked over, its owner or his man holding it on a halter and chatting between whiles with cronies and the characters who circulated. Another was to go to the 'ring', which in a horse market didn't mean what it now means in the antique business but to put a certain guarantee on the animals offered, since they had either been looked over and approved by the vet or would be sold subject to the vet's examination on behalf of the purchaser, the money being returned if anything seriously wrong was discovered. A man could advertise for a working horse of a certain age, mare, filly or gelding, broken to chains, cart and whatever else or he could visit the ring without buying a horse. Both advertising and visiting the ring and showing interest encouraged two sorts of horse copers, those who had a good animal and wanted the best possible price for it and those who thought they might pull the wool over some poor farmer who didn't know a broken-winded mare from an elephant.

The copers were great opportunists. They rarely put any horse they bought into the ring. They sometimes picked up bargains from owners who were hard-pressed and needed the money. They would then 'walk' the horse to sell it, much in the same way as the itinerant seller of pots, pans and cheap towels toured the countryside to sell at the doors of remote cottages and farms. A 'walked' horse was suspect, but the story that went with it always tended to smooth away suspicion. For a long time the chosen purchaser had been noted as a 'fine judge of an animal', a man who knew horses and, coming by a bargain (so-and-so was 'going out' and selling-off his working horses well in advance since he wouldn't be cultivating the land), the choice for first refusal had been obvious.

It sometimes worked. There was also the sad story of having had a bargain, an animal that was right for the ring and a price of maybe 40 guineas, but with a wife and children in imminent danger of being put out on the road—a compulsory sale! There was often a partnership in the business, two copers arriving on a cart with the mare to be sold in tow. One of the partners would be drunk and the other sober. The drunk one would be ready to give the horse away for a few pounds and his companion had to point out that a drunk man wasn't himself. To take the offer would be next to robbery. A switch in this line was the unreasonableness of the drunk and the willingness of the sober one.

When we wanted a working horse it generally came from the ring. It would be handled, walked, examined not only by the vet but by a relative who had been a high-class coper himself, buying mounts for the cavalry and touring Ireland, accumulating a string of shrewd purchases. Only once in a while did the copers come to the door. A man who bred Clydesdales wasn't likely to be misled about the quality of the animal he was offered without a vet's certificate, but I well remember when, out of the blue, two copers arrived in a car, driving not too fast for the mare that was tied behind.

Now they come jolting up the road with the mare's big feet splashing through the puddles and leaving them mud-coloured. The sun had come out. We saw them from a long way off and grandfather, who loved to talk about horses, plodded from the rickyard to the steps before the house to see his visitors draw up. They turned their battered car in the steading and brought it to a halt without so much as a glance at the mare in tow. One of them paid more attention to getting the door back on the ramshackle tourer before he came to bid us good-day. At fifty yards the mare showed her age. The copers grinned and came and shook hands. The breath of the distillery, a sort of bran flavour, the result of many wee 'halfs', glasses and drams, came with them. They accepted an invitation to have a cup of tea. No one mentioned the mare, but that was always the way of things. Selling the mare was the very last thing that would arise and the price would be discussed, negotiated like the Treaty of Versailles.

The talk was of bareness on turnip hills and milk sent back from the creamery because it hadn't been properly cooled, a wildcat taken in a trap somewhere up on the moors and the death of old Willie so-and-so who had been a market figure for a generation. Out in the court the mare stood patiently waiting. Hens picked their way beneath her belly, and the cock, flying up on to the old car, crowed loudly. After a cup of tea and a scone, the whisky bottle passed. At last came a small word, the repetition of the merest whisper of speculation, that we had need of a spare horse come harvest. Our brood mares were in foal, both Jess and Jean. True, true the mares were in foal, but not all the corn hills round about ripened in the same few days. We had relatives and neighbours with spare horses. There wasn't much to be said for a mare that threw one foot out badly and looked as though she had a tender shoulder. The failings and virtues of the mare were bandied about without either party even glancing out of the window. Her price was £25. There would be years of work in her yet. She was a steady, willing animal.

Her price fell, however. The depression settled on the copers as the clock chimed. It would soon be milking time and few farmers entertained horse-dealers in the evening. They had a long way to go home and the pace could hardly be smartened. Another tot of whisky did little to brighten the sky, although it reddened their cheeks. They knew that they were going to sell the mare. They even knew the price. There was a short while when I wondered about the outcome, however, for abruptly we were away considering the black cattle on the grass park outside the town, and the need for 'back-weeding' turnip rows. It came at last, however, the outstretched palm, the slap of hand on hand. We had a temporary working mare for harvest for £15. In due course, groomed, well-fed and doctored, re-shod to change her foot-throwing weakness, she would be sold in the market.

The copers took their money and spat on it as was the custom, before they tucked it into their wallets—£7 10s apiece. They looked at the whisky bottle just once before they rose and went to unhitch the mare from the old car. She wasn't a bad-looking beast. She was docile and good-tempered. Her teeth were good and she hadn't been ill-used, although she badly needed the curry and brush. We put her in the stable for the night, grandfather having run his hands over her legs, back and shoulders. She was a bargain. She wouldn't have been a bargain at three o'clock when the sun was shining and the cock crowing, but in the evening when the last of the swallows had come into the cartshed and the barn owl was flying along the hedge, she was a most useful acquisition at £15. Three or four months later she was sold for £25. The harvest was in by then, and there was no need for spare horses in the stable.

Memories of Cattle Shows

There are all sorts of enthusiasms that make the heart of one man or another beat faster. The sight of a hunt moving off, the white movement on a cricket pitch when the elms are softly rustling on a summer's afternoon, or the great cheer that goes up from a football field all have their effect on those who love such things. Apart from a glimpse of a stream passing beneath a stone bridge or a flight of duck streaming downwards towards a lake, my excitement is in seeing an agricultural show in progress, for I was brought up on agricultural shows. I know them from the inside and I know, too, the anticipation of the day, the tense hours of preparation, the free, light-hearted feeling among farming people when the bright day arrives somewhere between the beginning of summer and harvest. I don't have to go into the show field; I don't need to slow down as I pass. I can hear the announcements, the snigger of a horse, the bleat of sheep and the lowing of cows, even if I do no more than look at a tattered bill on some wall in the village. As I read of the event I sigh a nostalgic sigh for the milking competitions, the yellow-dyed ewes and the pony races I saw so often in my childhood because then, much more than to-day, a cattle show was a big event.

Every farmer in the district made a point of being at the show in the days when transport was mainly by pony and trap. It was one way of making contact with friends. One generation looked at the next and the old men looked anxiously for old companions. How often I heard my elders say of this or that old fellow: 'Well, he didn't look himself at the show. I had a feeling it might be his last,' and, when some one who had been missed for years was discovered prodding a pen of sheep or pigs with his walking stick: 'I declare to my God, I was afraid you were dead!' The talk on these occasions was endless. The gatherings enlarged and enlarged until they were forced to split again into more intimate groups that in turn grew into a congestion of friends and the friends of friends, first cousins and second cousins, relations and the relatives of relatives. I think I met most of my own distant relatives at shows and often stood as a child while they gazed into my face and compared the family likeness, measured me for size, brought forward their own sons and daughters and began comparing features anew. At such times I had a feeling that everyman was my kinsman and I looked fondly at people I had never seen before and smiled, now and then expecting to be claimed by a far-out uncle, a distant aunt or even the half-brother of the woman who came up to help with the milking!

'This is Bob's boy,' someone would say. 'A grandson of old John?' another would ask. A rough farmer's hand would take my own and I would look into a whiskered face that studied me for the dark eyes or the green eyes of one side of the family or the other. More often than not I was given a sixpence for ginger ale or gassy lemonade. This was one aspect of kinship I could never understand but never questioned. Once, expecting a coin, I was given instead the halter of a massive Clydesdale horse, which I had to mind while its owner went hurriedly ploughing into the crowd to find my father and pump his arm and talk of days gone. While they stood at a distance escaping into their boyhood and leaving me lost in the moving throng, the Clydesdale whisked his tail and tossed his head and I felt like a fly at the end of that great white tufted rope.

If the day of the show was a joyful occasion like a Sunday picnic, the night before was one of bustle and activity, of grooming, combing, soaping, washing and plaiting of manes and beribboning of tails. The whole pride of the family had to go into the preparation of a mare or a gelding, the perfect appearance of an Ayrshire cow with a bag on her that made walking ungainly and almost unnatural. The cows were usually walked to a farm near town on the eve of the show, fed a mash, watered and left until morning. The horses were kept in the stable, standing on clean straw in the light of a lamp as a mare might have spent the night of foaling. Everyone went early to bed at other times, but on that night preparation for the morrow was of prime importance. There was so much to be done before everyone could take a holiday. In the morning the horses went plodding away before milking time, with the horsemen warned to keep clear of puddles and to walk the animals on the grass verges, making sure that nothing made them panic and that they arrived at the show field comfortable and at ease.

After milking the trap was brought out, the pony harnessed and a last look taken at the appearance of the turn-out, for our brass had to sparkle and the harness shine like boned leather. There was rarely much opportunity for anyone to preserve his dignity as we journeyed, for we were nearly always too crowded in the trap, with every seat occupied and a child or two down in the well half-smothered in travelling rugs and nudged by many feet of all sizes. If the ploughman or his child stopped us on the way, then there was room for another. The pony was a sturdy, powerful animal, and he had to be. When we came to the town the trap quickly shed its load and trundled to the mews at the back of one of the hotels. Gigs and traps of all descriptions blocked the square and filled the back entries. Here and there stood a pony tethered to the wheel of a gig, with a great bag of oats to keep it content until its owner came back, but we always had a stable and a place to leave the trap in the cobbled mews. The town was alive that day as it was never alive on any other. The dogs no longer basked on the warm flags, for the foot traffic was thick and heavy. The Italian was not to be seen propping his red and yellow doorway as on other days, but he was inside his cool ice-cream parlour, serving for all he was worth and quarrelling with his wife in his native tongue with such vehemence that I used to think there might be a murder to add to all the other wonders of the cattle show.

At the gate of the field we paid our money and had our hands stamped with an indelible ink. The oval stamp was the sign to the gatekeeper when we sought re-entry in the afternoon after we had eaten a meal in one of the hotels of the town. I can remember so well the thrill it was to have that mark on my hand, although my mother protested that it made those who permitted it no better than the cattle in the pens within the field. Once in the ground we hurried to see our own entries, to study the mare and her foal and bolster ourselves with a conviction that the one in the next pen was not half so good, and knock-kneed and ugly-headed into the bargain. Sometimes when we arrived the preliminary judging had taken place. Red and blue tickets were about. We held our breath to see a red ticket. We smiled with pleasure at a blue one and shook our heads sadly at a commended animal, for it was plainly a bad day with the judges.

There was never such an occasion as this. Never so much fun and excitement, with the band playing noisily and out of tune, the parade of prizewinners and the jaunty men in riding kit hurrying about wearing their committee badges and organising a track for trotting and galloping, putting up poles for jumps and tall spruce for the event of the sports, the 'bending' race. The field was trodden and trampled by so many feet—some of them not so immaculate with shine and polish as they had been in the morning—that the smell of crushed grass filled the air, and although here and there a cartload of sheep jolted away, or a nervous gelding was led in a prancing side-stepping walk to the exit gate with an air that all was over, the tension mounted. People were forced on to and through the ropes as the crowd became anxious to see who was riding which pony and who was game and who was tame. The shout that went up at the start of the races often put the rooks out of the elms and made dogs bark in the backyards of the town. The cheers, the encouragement and betting cries drowned the thud of the horses' hoofs. Ladies who had earlier seemed restrained and dignified screamed, 'Come on, Jimmie!' and the boys yelled for the success of the smallest and roundest pony. 'Come on, the wee one! Come on!' I can hear it yet.

It had to end. The rooks went back to roost. The Italian sold his last ice-cream and pop and the gigs and traps went clattering out of town. The stragglers went along the roads begging for lifts and here and there we overtook cows and horses being conveyed back to their farms. How tired we were! What a blissful day it had been, and hadn't old James been full of the devil and wasn't Sarah looking well?

I hardly ever go near a cattle show now. I'm not so well up in the latest mechanical wonders that take up so much space at the show. Since life goes at an altogether faster pace today I hardly imagine that there are many country people who meet as infrequently as we did, but when I see a dressed-up groom and a horse with ribbons in his mane and tail, my mind goes back to yesterday and a lot of people who were old when I was a boy.

The Killing of a Hill Fox

No one seemed particularly elated at the end of that long, cold spring day when the fox was carried down the mountain by the root of his tail, his legs dangling, his tongue lolling and his bright eyes closed for ever. But the hill shepherds were pleased—they had talked about this fox for a long time and worked up a hate for him that allowed of no sentimentality. Yet if the shepherds had taken vengeance the remainder of the party had the guilt of assassins, even those whose guns were innocent of the smell of burnt powder. I had been a spectator and unarmed (unless a fly-rod in a bag could be construed to be a weapon). To me the whole thing was a sort of ambush. The fox had had no chance. There had been a bounty on his head, for he had taken a score of lambs, they said. Perhaps one of the shepherds claimed the reward, but the fox, I felt, should have been killed somewhere else than on the screes where the buzzard sails and the peregrine hunts.

The hills have always had a mystical influence, so far as I am concerned, and an atmosphere of peace that, like the surface of a pool, shouldn't be disturbed by stone-throwing or gunfire. My imagination stirred when I considered that party with their old guns, their soil-stained coats tied at the waist with twine and their varied sorts of headgear—they looked like brigands on some far-eastern frontier. The fox had, after all, been running the trails he had always run on the mountain where he had been whelped; a Welsh mountain not a raven's flight from the place in which I now live.

It began early in the morning. There was a chill breeze in the valley, and lingering shadows and mist down in the trees along the river. The stones on the rough road leading to the hill track were cased in frost and marked by the boots of the shepherds as they plodded upwards in small groups. They passed between the thorn hedges and the clumps of stunted birch trees and went on to the gorse and the more isolated rowans that dotted the lower slope of the mountain.

Hill shepherds never seem to hurry; the company moved at the same steady pace that it would have taken at shearing time or when any of them were looking their flocks in high summer, but they carried their guns with an unfamiliarity that betrayed their use of sticks and crooks on normal occasions. They talked about the price of lambs and grazing, who had done well and who had failed. Sometimes they collided with one another on the rough track and laughed even when the barrels of their shaky guns rang.

The ridge was an hour or two away and the job would take all day unless they were extraordinarily lucky. As they progressed from the last gate towards the ridge, men dropped out one by one to take their allotted places. The county pest officer had been enlisted to secure the co-operation of as many guns as possible, and he, too, plodded on until the last landmarks could be pointed out and identified for the benefit of those who were not men of the hills. I went right to the ridge, having abandoned my plan to go and fish one of the little pools away over to the east. They said the fox would never get to the ridge, no matter on which side he was flushed.

When we got to the top, my companion (a taciturn fellow) sat down in the shelter of a rock and fell into contemplation. I looked down the slope that I had climbed. From the ridge, it was impossible to see both slopes because of the nature of the ground, but on the slope that I could see I noted the next man down sitting on a sack beside a mound. Perhaps a

61

quarter of a mile beyond him another man stood in a sort of ruined temple of slate slabs. We were a chain of assassins marking the fox's way to the ridge, and it was the same on the slope above the next valley. Once the terriers and mongrel pack moved the fox from the security of his rocky hiding places, 20 or 30 guns would menace him. Without the pack the fox might have slipped through, but with the pack on his trail he would have small chance of slipping away. He would short-cut the trail and cross open ground.

When I thought about it I understood why the time had come. The hill was bare. The bracken wasn't up and the round rushes on the boggy shelves were bleached. The wethers had cropped everything away at the onset of winter and the cover was poor indeed. I sighed for him and waited. They would whistle and wave once he was on his way, and until that moment the assassins would stand or sit like stone images. I was the only odd man in the field. Since I had brought no gun to the ridge I was under suspicion, I felt. I dared not shout nor wave my hat—when the time came—to send the fox off his trail and along the mountain instead of over it. They were banking on him running his few trails to the top and they would hold their fire until he was well within lethal range.

Morning wore to noon, and noon towards evening. What little warmth the pale yellow sun had given was quickly carried away by the breeze. The terriers far below had worked through countless clusters of rock and endless tunnels of slate, when all at once a whistle was sounded. My companion picked up his battered field-glasses and scanned the ground.

'He crossed the boggy bit a minute ago,' he said.

I took the glasses when they were offered. A mile below me a man was waving his arms. Then I saw the fox, his brush trailing on the ground as he angled upwards towards the next shoulder of rock following the sheep track. I wondered how long it would be before he ran into one of the guns. I did not have long to wait for an answer: the report of the shot echoed off the lower crags and there was a long silence before half a dozen men appeared in different places and began to wave their arms. The whistle blew—a long shrill note. The ambush had worked. The fox was dead.

Men from the other side of the ridge appeared on the skyline and called through their cupped hands. One waved his cap in a slow circling motion before they went back. I used my rod as a staff and went down the slope. The man lower down stayed back to keep us company and we hurried on to come up with some of the others. We were in groups of three or four by the time we came to the gate and the road, and ahead of us was the man with the lamb-killing fox. We came up with him at the place from which we had started. He had thrown the fox on to a bank as evidence for all to see.

'He won't do it no more,' he said.

It seemed an unnecessary remark, and I was glad that among that armed company I alone had not been a party to the killing.

A Grand Harvest Day

A starling piping on the chimney opposite reminded me of a remark often used in my boyhood, 'It's a grand harvest day.' Harvest was a long way away, of course, but that old comment on the beauty of a morning went well with the song of the starling, the sunlight touching the beech tree, the out-of-season, high, blue heavens and the sound of the stream. Sometimes we used the expression ironically when the firwood up the hollow was obscured in driving rain and the barrel at the byre gable overflowed and made a stream in the court, but generally the words were used for the kind of morning that uplifted the heart and made the most unmusical want to sing whether harvest was at hand or not.

At some time every summer, between May and September, it was remarked that it was a grand harvest day. Perhaps the corn was still green, perhaps we stood on the peat moss watching the cotton grass swaying, perhaps the morning sun glinted on the river and a big trout rose in the pool below the bridge, but there was a wonderful mixture of delight and relief when the harvest day arrived and the oats had turned yellow and the breeze rustled the tall corn. That day began before milking time when the air was chill, fields were wet with dew and the last star was lingering above the turnip-field. It began when the kitchen door opened and one of the family stepped out to take a breath of air, listening to the whispering of small birds and glancing up to see a solitary curlew going westwards after the retreating night. Across the court the family of cats would come running from barn and cartshed for their plate of porridge and milk, the collie dog would stalk stiffly to report for work and, at the sounds of activity, the hens would begin to croon and talk among themselves as the light filtered through the cobwebs and dust of the fowlhouse window.

At milking, those who expected to be recruited for work in the field would speculate about the heavy dew, but without doubt about the weather ahead, for when such a day dawned there was no denying that it had been born for harvest. There was no cloud. The hills were not magnified by humid air, but lying low, defined by the sun coming up behind them with the brilliance of a mass of marigolds. Before the dew had started to lift one knew that the straw would crackle at noon and the grasshoppers sing when waistcoats were draped over stooks, and the pail of meal and water was almost empty.

Above my bed there used to hang a picture of Ruth and Naomi in the harvest field. The picture was full of sunlight. The gleaners were there, and strange, Egyptian-looking harvesters cut the corn with sickles. There was something very foreign and Oriental about the people in the field, but the corn was the same, the scene familiar, for the artist had stood in a field of oats on a grand harvest day and set his scene. It was a pity he had had to put those outlandish headdresses on the brown-faced harvesters when I knew the background so well, for I might have enjoyed his work more had he shown me Wee Jimmie and Bella and Maggie stooking, Mick the Irishman laying back the sward with a long pole and Clyde and Mary stamping beside old Jean as the binder went perilously across the big hill, thrusting out sheaves at every yard.

When the dog had barked the milking cows back to the pasture everyone and everything seemed to move towards the field of corn. One man carried the knives in their wooden case, another a scythe and sharpening stone, a rake, a fork, a length of chain, a rope. These and other things went with Mick O'Hare and Daniel Kelly, imported harvesters from 'across the water,' Bella, the lass from the roadend, the team of Clydesdales and their jingling trace chains. 'Put a step on, boys,' someone would urge and the pace would quicken until feet were among the stubble and the dew-drenched clover undergrowth. The canvas of a binder cannot be risked on wet corn, the knives would clog, the knotter fail to work, so that the most eager harvest team has to await the smile of the sun to take the dew away and dry the fine grass at stubble height. Once the dew had gone the binder would begin to move. Sometimes a tilting reaper worked as well where the corn had folded over with the wind. Jack would swing his scythe to open awkward corners, Mick run with his pole to keep the heads from the horses' feet, and young and old, wearing mittens to save their hands from thistles, would toss sheaves back and stook. The sight of the bobbing heads of three strong Clydesdales in a binder thrills me yet. Often I sat up there, handling the lines and raising the knifeboard above protruding boulders. Often I worked the tilting reaper and sang to my heart's content, for no one could hear my voice in the clatter of the machine.

There was no escape on such a day. The sun might bless a hill of gorse, or the dry-stone wall might be a place in which a man could doze, listening with only half an ear to the distant noise of the cutting and the voices of the stookers, but no one was allowed to stretch in the scent of the gorse or sleep in the shade of the wall. Too many days of the year the grey clouds rolled up out of the south-west and hid the hills. Too often in the past had the stooks rooted and the uncut corn turned black, fit only to be ploughed in, like weeds. When the sun climbed a cloudless heaven and the cattle sought the shelter of the thorn hedge, it was not a day for dreaming, but a day for toil.

In the field the hardest workers were the Irishmen, for they made a contract and hoped to finish early on one farm to make a new contract on another where the ripening of the corn was late. Tea would come at mid-morning, tea in blue cans, scones from a big round basket. The binder stopped and the horses tugged at the heads of sheaves while the driver balanced scone on one hand and a bowl of hot tea on the other, but often the Irishmen worked on while the sun rose and glared upon the whitewash of farms along the course of the river. The hot rays scorched the sheep pasture, turning it from fawn to brown, but no one had time to do more than glance at a neighbour's harvesting. Willie would brush the perspiration from his eyebrows, and examine his palm for a thorn, but have no chance to remove it before the tilting reaper was round again, laying out more sheaves to be tied.

By late afternoon no one would remark about the harvest day. Backs would be sore, arms stung with the butts of sheaves and clothing sticking to backs already uncomfortable with the dust and little seeds of the field. The horses plodded on, the Irishmen looked for a rising moon so that, with a change of horses, the cutting could go on into the night until the dew fell again. The ripening was not always at harvest moon, however, and those who were weary longed for the quietness of the kitchen, the coolness of the water in the pump trough and the luxury of a chaff bed. Tomorrow the mist might come over from the sea or the hills sit with a curtain of cloud above them, but everyone was too exhausted to think much of tomorrow. Some would be half asleep at the supper table, fumbling with the last oatcake and slab of cheese, or absently stirring a cup of tea while the court outside filled with shadow and bats flew to and from the stable.

The workers who did not sleep in the loft would go back to their cottages, plodding down the road together in the darkness. Now and then one might pause to scratch some uncomfortable spot between his shoulders, for a fragment of straw can make the wearing of a shirt a devilish discomfort, and his companions would call, 'Haste you home, Tam. The old man will be lookin' for his harvest the morn, and your bed's cryin' for you!'

On the hill the binder would sit under a sheet, waiting for the cutting to begin again. All the sheaves would be stooked. The knives would be back at the steading to be sharpened before the dew lifted on a new harvest day. That did not always mean tomorrow, but a morning when the swallows were high. The first of the family to awaken would lift a skylight, peer out at the night and say, sleepily, 'Come on, get up, it's a grand harvest day!' and the day of stooping and straightening, lifting and tying, would begin again, with everyone making a little prayer that it would soon be over and those who had to work in the field might find life less strenuous in the black earth among the potatoes with an autumn breeze about them.

Death of a Little Railway

Some years ago I wrote a sort of requiem for a train, the *Paddy*, on which I had so often travelled from Euston to Galloway. The *Paddy* came to the end of its nightlong haul on the quay at Stranraer where it unloaded passengers for the Irish boat. Turning this piece up the other day, and musing about the way it had once been, it struck me that a whole little railway system had operated in Galloway and had died without my ever saying a valedictory word about it. The Old Wigtown-

66

shire Railway (railway buffs will know that the word Portpatrick was at one time included because it served that port among others) carried the first railway engine I ever saw.

Children born and brought up in towns generally get to know the railway engine from their prams, but my first experience of the train was the sounds it made when miles away across the undulating farmland of Galloway. On wet days the sound was hollow. When the winter winds swept the Machars, hardening the land and stopping the plough, the sound was churning and sharp, while in summer, on a warm afternoon, it was drowsy as the sound of honey-drunk bees. I knew the piping of the whistle. Sometimes I caught a brief glimpse of a plume of smoke, and then I saw the thing, at last, when I was taken to the station to watch it arrive. It was one of the great wonders of a world of innocence. I still remember the heat that radiated from the engine and see those dragon's breath gusts of steam drifting down the platform, on to which churns were dumped with coils of wire and cans of Archangel tar for the treatment of footrot in sheep.

I know the excitement my grandfather must have felt when the single track was built in his remote part of the country. He had once thought to join the staff. I understood my father's heavy heart as the train hurried him off from the beauty of that place to the awful tenement lodgings he had to take while learning to be an engineer. That whole railway system, tendril by tendril, wilted and died in the end, but once its minor branches had reached out to make links with far-off romantic places—Edinburgh, and even London if anyone had the inclination to go so far.

I came into the world too late to enjoy an opportunity to take a train to one of the ports served by a 'steam and sailing vessel' called the *Countess of Galloway*. This fine ship plied between the country of my infant nurture and Liverpool, carrying a mixed cargo of cattle goods and venturesome countryfolk. Long before I might have contemplated such a trip the *Countess* had gone to the breaker and her commander, a Mr James Coid, had swallowed the anchor. I could have run down to Whithorn, but only to take a pleasure cruise to the Isle of Man on *Mona's Queen*. The railway played a large part in our comings and goings while it continued in use. It changed its name, however, when it was absorbed by the LMS, and perhaps this was when its days began to be numbered, but I travelled on its slender tendril from Newtown Stewart down the Machars unaware that change was taking place.

I came again and again, bleary-eyed at the end of a journey from Euston to Newtown Stewart to await my connection there. Often I stood on the frost-crusted platform listening to the rooks awakening in the rookery above the station master's house and watching the dawn climb the back of the Galloway hills. Cattle that spent the night in the market pens lowed and bellowed until they were sometimes brought at a gallop, soiling the road to the yard of the station. The train that eventually came to meet me would rattle and rock through a magic world of early morning in which shadowy birds flew and sheep went bumping off into the safety of gorse or heather. The train might have been some kind of prehistoric monster preying daily on the flocks.

That this old railway could die, without my ever being aware that it was coming to its dotage, puzzles me now. I had little news of it in the years of my absence, but once there was a disaster between Newtown Stewart and Burrow Head beyond Whithorn, where the artillery fired on Queen Bee planes to sharpen crews for the blitz. Some hopeful officer hurried his artillery piece down the line without enquiring about bridge clearances or checking the elevation of his gun. A bridge was so badly damaged, I was told, that the milk from shoreward farms could not be got to the creamery on the other side of the railway. What a calamity that must have been, and I missed it.

I missed too, the last journey of rusty, skim-milk churns, roofing felt, coals and chicken coops that went down the line. I sigh to think I did, for there an era ended. It had begun for me when I was less than five years old. The gig in which I was huddled in travelling rugs suddenly went at breakneck speed out of the station yard as the engine of the train groaned in agony, its drive wheels spinning and ringing on icy rails. I knew then that there was something more frightening than a runaway and even more powerful than a rearing Clydesdale stallion. Nothing has ever impressed me quite as much since.

Journey to the Mill

We grew some very good barley and oats when I was a boy. The barley was for the distillery, and the oats were either sold, or 'bruised'—rough milled—to be fed to cattle and hens as mash. The horses consumed a lot of oats too. I suppose the occasional small acreage of rye went to the mill. Once or twice, between harvests, we took oats to the mill, and this was a very special occasion, for we came back with flour and oatmeal to replenish the meal 'ark' that stood in the corner of the kitchen, housing the great, fat-bellied sacks and keeping their contents in perfect condition. A porridge pot was never off the range. The men would help themselves to porridge before they went out in the early morning to catch up a ploughing team or bring in the milking herd. There was always a large white can of milk on hand, and they would help themselves to a bowl of milk at the same time. The stirring of the porridge pot was a continual chore for someone. Once in a while my grandmother would look in the ark to check on the remaining bulk of flour and oatmeal. With the baking of soda scones, and the daily making of porridge, both sacks tended to diminish. Towards the end, whoever dipped into them would almost be standing on his or her head, and it would be said more than once that it was time to go to the mill.

Going to the mill involved some preliminary operations. The best corn was stored in the high barn or granary. It was hard, clean grain, but of course, having only been through the winnowing drum of our built-in threshing mill, or a similar compartment of the steam threshing mill that came up to demolish the ricks, converting them in the process into great 'sow' stacks of straw and scores of sacks of oats, this threshed corn still had among it the seeds of the fields. In the high granary we had a machine, a hand-operated affair, which we called the fanner. It was more than a mere winnowing machine, for incorporated in its wooden walls were screens of different sizes, all of them inclined so that the grain would roll down them. These screens had a sort of reciprocating action, and when the big handle was turned the oats danced and were sieved; straw ends, fragments of minute stalks and so on, being held back and the fine seeds of things like thistles or dock being quickly filtered through the lowest and finest of the screens. On the way, the best oats rolled off into a chute and were bagged up. The tail corn emerged a little lower down.

The seeds of weeds were scattered inside the shed, where the free-range hens quickly devoured them. Those they didn't take a population of sparrows and almost tame finches quickly discovered. The tail corn was doled out to the hens over a period, or bruised to make mash, but the best oats went to the mill.

The sacks were tied with twine and lowered on a wheel chain to the cart that was trundled up to be loaded. Sometimes the cart was simply supported by a fence post across a milk churn, but when things were well organised, the loading took place when we were yoked and ready to make the journey to the mill. There was then no longer any need to leave the cart with a tarpaulin covering to protect the precious grain.

We grew no wheat. So many sacks of best oats were traded for so many sacks of best wheat flour. The wheat was imported. We never saw it as grain, even at the mill. A lot of reciprocal trading went on. Barley went to the distillery and the carts carrying it came back full of bran, which was excellent for feeding pigs. Milk went to the creamery, and often the cart that carried it held two or three churns to be filled with sour or skimmed milk, another highly-prized pig-fattener. Even if we hadn't intended to use the oatmeal at home, the corn taken to the mill would have been carefully selected and fanned or winnowed, for the quality of the crop was a matter of great pride.

Whenever I could contrive to persuade the carter to take me, I went to the mill. It was a great adventure to sit perched on the fore-end of the cart as it slowly rocked and jolted its way along the road to the mill in the nearest village. The road wound past farms I knew well. I could look down on cottage gardens and see hens fluffing themselves in the potato rows, or cats basking in the warm sun. I could feel superior to the cottage children who ran alongside admiring the great Clydesdale horse, or horses, if we either had two carts or used tracing horses. I loved the length of road that went through the moss.

The scent of myrtle was strong. Sometimes a cock grouse got up on the wall before he went clattering away out into the wilderness that had once been a birch wood. The journey took an hour or two. It was never long enough. I was always conscious of the sound of the axle, the creaking of the sideboards or rails, the rattle of the iron wheelrims on the boulders, and the sound of the chains as the horse held back the load on some steep hill.

The mill was a flour-dusty place. The miller seemed permanently aged by the flour that whitened his hair. The noise was endless, for it seemed that the millstones never stopped; and indeed, although they might not be grinding, they never ceased revolving so long as water was in the sluice. The very floor of the building vibrated. Half the conversation of those who transacted business there was lost in the rumble of the gear. The miller was an expert lip-reader, but that hardly helped the carter, who had been told to bring back some special information about the quality and price of corn that year.

It didn't take long to get the milling done. The miller's loading platform, a great stone structure projecting from the side of the building, was equipped with a sort of swinging gantry and a very large wheel, so that the milled corn could be dropped exactly where it was needed without any strenuous hauling or struggling with the tightly-filled and dusty sacks. The journey home took just as long, but like most return journeys, it never seemed so long. I enjoyed the scene just as much on the way back. I loved the smell of fields of swedes, the sight of a goldfinch on a thorn tree, or a hare making off across a meadow, gathering speed with one ear down first, and then both slicked on his neck as away he went at full gallop. The carter was always glad to get back for his dinner.

Salt beef, new potatoes and buttermilk it might be, or rabbit pie. Nothing I have tasted since ever went down better. One's tastes, like life itself, were simple and wholesome. The flour we brought home wasn't bleached; the oats had never been treated with any sort of spray. Weeds grew in the corn but we had greenfinches, chaffinches, goldfinches round the steading, and a milling throng of sparrows, house sparrows and tree sparrows, to pick the chaff.

Rat-catching Days

Our local rat-catcher went past a little while ago with a terrier at his heel and a can hooked on his arm. He always carries a can of bait when out on his job. Sometimes I stop and have a word with him, for he is something of an expert, and while he has a bit of what might be called technical jargon and all the scientific advice the official pamphlets can provide, he has a sort of affection for his quarry and knows a great deal about them.

'Now there's sewer rats an' bakehouse rats, warehouse rats an' rick rats,' he remarked to me once. 'I can tell 'em all, an' you got to be able to tell 'em or it takes longer to get 'em.' I suppose there is some sort of difference in rats that feed and live in different places. There seemed a distinct difference between the rats I once saw in a slaughterhouse and those that lived in the vicinity of a near-by chicken run. We had rat runs across our garden once when old Sam along the way kept chickens. I saw one of these chicken-run rats that seemed to be ready to leave a litter in a heap of hedge cuttings at the end of the garden and foolishly decided to smoke her out. A heavy downpour of rain was all that saved me from the ignominy of having to call a fire brigade to put out a blaze that enveloped the hedge and fence.

Jack, the rat-catcher, would never have approved my methods, and my neighbours thought that I had gone a bit far almost to burn the place down for the sake of ridding myself of a rat. From that day on they regarded me as a little eccentric over rats, as well as over the jackdaws which nested in our chimneys.

My earliest attempt at dealing with rats took place a long time ago. A

71

place near my grandfather's farm went up in flames, and shortly afterwards it was discovered that a plague of rats had come upon us. In no time they were gnawing at the granary door, skittering along the beams in the stable, undermining the flags in the barn and nesting in every corner and crack as well as in corn chests and troughs. My grandfather was dismayed. The movement of rats was a bad sign for those whose premises they left, a plague to those chosen by the rats to provide a new home. I offered to organise a harrying party. I formed a sort of rat hunt over which I was master. The hounds were two collies. I also found a polecat ferret to assist. I armed my huntsmen with cudgels and planned forays with an eye to tactics and strategy.

It was October when we began to hunt. The experts had had their day. They had been along with their gas and their baits. They had stopped holes, pumped gas into the buildings, baited, lured and trapped, and they had made as much impression on the rat tribe as a charge of dust fired at a greylag goose. Of the two collies, Help, the elder, was a poor advertisement for his name, but Jackie, the young dog, had the devil in him and killed faster than a terrier. He went in like a tiger, crossing the barn floor and tossing rats up as fast as he could open and close his lean, white-fanged jaws. There were times when he almost knocked me off my feet as, with storm lanterns held ready and cudgels gripped in our hands, we threw back a door and charged in to kill as many as we could. At that time rat tails were paid for at the rate of twopence each. A bag of thirty or forty rats in a night was not uncommon and yet the great tribe never seemed a whit smaller. They got through our defences and spoiled and devoured corn and cattle food. They had found secret ways through the old stone buildings, recesses and cavities that no one had noticed before. They scurried in the cheese loft, scuttled over heaps of grass rope, dived under the winnowing machine and bolted through the workings of the threshing mill and continued to breed and breed until one saw their whiskered faces and beady eyes everywhere.

I remember one night when we killed over a hundred. To save the chicken food a quantity of tail corn and winnowings had been tipped into an old cheese vat in the barn. The vat was about sixteen feet in length, about five feet wide and over two feet deep. Someone had carelessly left a corn sack hanging on the end of the vat and the rats used this sack as a way in and out of the vat. When I discovered this fact I tied a long rope to the sack and carried the rope to the outside of the barn door. It was a simple matter to come along at night, pull the rope and draw the sack out of the vat, which automatically trapped the rats feeding in the corn. The rope was left lying under the door, after a test

72

had been made to ensure that all was in working order, and later that night, with the hounds beside us, we came on tiptoe to the barn, pulled the rope and went in to look at the catch. The floor of the vat swarmed with rats that continually sprang up to escape and slithered down the metal. Before we could stop him the young collie was in the midst, killing while the rats clung to his coat and hung thick on his neck and sides. We could not go into the vat because its frame was supported on wheels and its thin base would burst under our weight. We killed the trapped rats as humanely as we could. The collie that straddled them on the bottom of the vat killed more than three men together, and when the last rat was accounted for we thought we had made a worth-while reduction of the plague.

Alas, we were mistaken in thinking the rats might be under control. In a night or two we found them as numerous as ever. I obtained a pistol and used to sit on a sack of corn with a lamp at my boots and the boots well greased so that the smell attracted the rats. When, after a minute or two of waiting, the rats began to venture out across the floor to sniff and nibble at my boots, I used to take aim with the pistol. The range was short and the lamp, being close to my boots, made accuracy fairly certain. Each time I killed a rat the others would rush for their holes. I waited until they recovered their nerve and came out again, which they did within a few minutes. I shot a few score of rats in a month by this method, but I often wondered what might have happened had I been so unwary as to fall asleep. Sometimes I would go into the stable with a lamp in my hand, aim the pistol at a particular place in the beams and shoot when a rat came into my sights as they always did when bolting through the rafters.

There were nights when the polecat ferret did his work, following the runs and driving the grey multitude before him, but there were others when the ferret backed out with bloody jaws and the signs of battle upon him. After a while, when he had fought some of the crop-eared old warriors of the stone runs and under-floor tunnels, the ferret refused to hunt. His taste for battle was no more.

The rats continued to hold their own. They bred their freaks and sickly ones. They had among them three-legged veterans, wheezy-chested, half-blind old rick rats that lived in odd corners, and there was no keeping them down. The gas experts said the holes were too numerous. The poison experts said it was impossible to deny enough of the rats access to food. They did their best, but it was useless. I invented a swing-door trap and baited it with a bit of kipper. The trap used to be packed with prisoners in the morning and I used to carry it out and submerge the whole thing in a water barrel. Day after day of rat-catching made no impression and we began to see that more passive means were the only way. When the wood at the side of a door was eaten through we replaced it with iron-shod timber. When flags began to rock and become unsafe we took up floors and put down concrete. The corn chests were made rat-proof. Uprights were fitted with rat-excluding skirts of tin, and where holes were found they were filled with cement. We listened to a deal of advice but did no more to contain the plague. One day, said my grandfather, the plague would leave us. The rats would breed themselves out. We were not in favour of a barbaric plan to singe a rat and send the poor scorched creature back into the runs to put the fear of fire in the others. We were not in favour of witchcraft, charms or spells. As the women who came up to milk said, when the power that sent the plague was ready, it would take it away again, and things happened like that. The rats vanished.

I came home on holiday about a year later. The rats? Oh, the rats had gone. No one could say exactly when or how. We had no rats now and was that not something to be thankful for? Whether they died or migrated I never discovered. When I talked to our local rat-catcher he was not at a loss for an answer. The king rat had led them away. There was always a king and when rats swarmed over a place for years there came a moment when the king craved a change. It was always so. As to the methods of the experts and my huntsmen, well, we deserved to keep rats if we couldn't get rid of them.

On Being Able to Plough

'And can you plough?' used to be a leading question to the lad who came seeking a job at term day, for a second ploughman was an asset about a place and a lad who could not plough was like a horse that had never been broken to shafts. I doubt whether the question is often put now. There are fewer horses, fewer horse-ploughs and far fewer young men who can manage either. The question asked is one about tractors and mechanics and the answer involves turning circles and gear ratios.

It is a sad thing. I see a certain sadness reflected in the faces of the old farmers at market, the bearded ones with out-of-fashion, high-buttoned waistcoats, silver watch chains and hard black boots. There are times when I have a strong inclination to stop one of them and ask if he wants a man to plough an acre or two in the traditional way, for, although I have next to none of the social graces and few gifts, I can plough. I can plough hill or hollow, hoof-hammered pasture or soft bog. I can talk to horses and sing a bit of a tune while the gulls flutter and sink and sail behind me and the freshly turned earth shines with the iron-mark of the blade. A little time has passed since I did so, it is true, but I have the way of the plough and have turned thousands of acres in my imagination since last my hands were upon the stilts.

More than twenty years ago I ploughed a field of black earth, earth like a peat bog, sheltered by tall trees of pine and fir and bounded by a ditch where the meadow-sweet grew and perfumed the air in summer. I was visiting a relative who farmed there and offered my hand to his plough when his man went sick. A dark Irish horse plodded at my side and a mare trailed a little behind as I took the pair to the field, down the hard road and through the trees to the bridge across the ditch. The plough was yoked. The team stood waiting. I turned the lines about my wrists, gripped the handles and urged the pair forward. The black earth turned as I walked with the ploughman's limp along that furrow. I was set about the serious business of ploughing, ploughing straight and true, ploughing at an even depth, sparing the shoulders of my team by riding a sunken boulder, sparing my ribs by clinging to the stilts as the coulter plunged and buried the sock too deep. Any man with might and main can hold a plough for a single furrow and pretend that the wavering is no more than the contour of the land, but when furrow lies on furrow and the day is wearing away, when breath is steam and pigeons are clattering in to roost, it must all lie true and even like parings of cheese. There is no other way.

The earth of this field was black and heavy. It was deep and rich, a place for growing potatoes or oats, if only sufficient sun came to ripen the crop. In the late afternoon someone arrived with a basket and a tea can. I straightened my back and let the team stand. A robin fed on the furrow and in the wood a wren sang sadly. Yes, they agreed, I was making a hand of it. I was ploughing. It was not my first hour at the plough, but it was my first spell alone in a field, plodding the furrow, my own critic, judge of my own mistakes.

The tea can went back to the farm-house and I set myself to finish the day. The horse and the mare sometimes had their heads together and showed a tendency to stand at the headland until ordered to turn in. I had to coax and cajole them and look often at what I had done to keep heart enough to continue. Blue mist was in the trees up on the hills and far-away sheep were bleating comfort to one another when I stopped the pair with the plough at the opening of a new furrow. I had done enough and I went home to the farm, to supper and a soft chaff bed.

In the morning I was back again, driving a pheasant from the field and putting rabbits to their warren in the wood. My arms had the ache of yesterday in them. My back was stiff and my song less spontaneous, but already I had turned the ground to grow enough oats to keep a man or a horse for many days, and I was no longer trying my hand at ploughing for amusement. Mick and Mary knew me as they had not known me before, and I knew their ways. When Mick tossed his head he crowded Mary and her foot broke the furrow and when Mary was allowed rein she would nip her partner's neck or shoulder. When I rested at the headland, the pair rested too, and it was bad for all of us to rest too long, listening to a cart jolting on some distant road, or a hoarse cock's crow. 'Mick! Mary! Out of that!' and we were away with the thorn bush appearing between their bobbing heads and serving as a mark, a steering point in a sea of an untidy field being turned into black waves.

Later, when the ploughman recovered his health, and I left the field, I went home and ploughed again. I made a head-rig scratch, marked out an old pasture that was to have two years of grain and one of roots, and broke the virgin soil. This field was not black but brown. It rose and fell. Snipe fed in its lower corner where water collected. Seagulls found me as I ploughed and came from the farthest corners of the heavens, and I toiled hour after hour along the rocky hillocks, up the slopes and down the brows, breaking the hare's bed, plunging through the mole's tunnels and wrecking the home of the mouse. The morning sun made the earth steam and in the evenings the moist furrows seemed to congeal, ready for the hardening of the night's frost. Partridges rose and sailed round my team as I led them home and the fresh wind from the hills ruffled my hair and cooled my brow. 'How is it shaping in the Old Road Field?' they asked when I came from the stable and talked of single-trees and double-trees and chains and coulters and socks and wheel pins and the stubborn way of an old ploughmare wearing a stable mate's collar that rubbed her shoulder.

There is a timelessness about ploughing, and there is something in the nature of a field that shows the way of men long dead. The headlands and the drains tell the story of cultivation and a man ploughing looks at the same marks his predecessors used, eyes the same stones in the dry-stone wall, the same boulders on the land, the same ancient hills. He sees the same autumn and spring skies, and the call of the plover and the curlew are as timeless as the air and broken earth. Time has run away with me since I ploughed and listened to the creak of the hames and collar and the sound of the coulter breaking the turf before the ploughshare, but I have ploughed a great deal in reverie. I stand looking at the little fields flanking some of the valleys of Wales and imagine myself breaking them for a crop of oats or swedes. It is a thing one can do on a bright sunny morning in spring or while hanging on a gate listening to a pheasant calling in the hollow when autumn is in the wood and the stubble is bleached and old.

Once or twice in a season I stand and watch a team of horses and a plough, and I have been tempted to ask the ploughman to let me try my hand, but who would believe that one grown soft could hold a plough for as much as a yard? Would it not be a waste of time when every day, every hour is important to a man turning a field over with a plough drawn by horses?

On my walks through the fields I occasionally find an unattended plough lying behind a hedge. I look round to make sure my eccentricity is unobserved and then step between the handles, turn the implement and eye its set and line. If I feel safe enough I cock it up and put the coulter to the earth and call an imaginary team to attention. 'Prince, Jean, get on there!' I exclaim and watch the tall thorn on the far side of the field. Prince and Jean step forward, the chains tighten, the traces snap and swing and we are away.

It is a foolish sort of a dream, you think? Sometimes it goes so far as to cover an emergency when we have no more oil for our tractors and people are looking about for aged Clydesdales or Shire horses and men who can plough, for I am proud to think that I can plough, proud and happy. After all, it is a thing our ancestors did when the wooden plough was drawn by an ox and the scrub was low on the hills and the wolf ran in the shadow of the trees. Like thatching and rick-building and working in iron, it is a dying art and the world will regret it when the last of us, even the day-dreaming amateurs, have gone.

When the Birds Begin to Flock

Although the month of September is often notable for dry weather and Indian summer lingering on into October, acute drought at this time isn't usual. The marshy places in my part of the world rarely dry up and they become hard to walk upon. The weeds of shallow drains and ditches don't often wither and die back, especially the evergreen vegetation that birds and fowl frequenting these places habitually use as cover. This year it was different. We basked in warm sunshine. One or two earlier downpours had ensured the swelling of fruit. There were fine blackberries to ripen all along the hedges. The harvest had got off to a bad start because of that early rain, but once the combines got to work they soon transformed the fields of barley and oats to stubbles. While this was happening there were curlews on the fields that had been cut for hay or foraged by the machines that make a sort of green blizzard as they blow the grass into the container they trundle behind them. Duck flew to and fro at evening, flying in broad daylight at first, as they always do, and then gradually adopting the habit of coming in just at twilight, for once they are harried by guns even the young summer duck learn to be more cautious.

I walked some of the stubbles for partridges. There were good coveys here and there. A lot of birds rose, but most of them were close to the root fields and the weedy furrows where insects were plentiful, and the dust-bathing was good. I remarked upon the dryness of the ditches, and the hardness of the ground where yellowing round rushes grew. The streams were low, and coming to them I noticed that birds that might normally have hidden in the bankside growth were below that level. Instead of heading for the bank, moorhens and coots either paddled off at speed along the middle of the waterway or flapped into the air and scuttled downstream, disturbing the slowly flowing water with their trailing legs or heavily beating wings. I didn't see teal where there might have been teal because clumps of duckweed and cress had shrunk and blackened.

About this time I noticed that the curlews were gathering early. Curlews always leave the inland places and the hayfields for the coastal fields at this time of year. It is a natural migration brought on by a gradual hardening of the weather, a fall in temperature which reduces the amount of food on more exposed areas and sometimes makes the boring and searching of long-beaked birds such as curlews and snipe more arduous than they care to have it. They go where the climate is milder. The rich ground of well-watered pastures and salt marshes, where cattle feed, provides a daily banquet. Along the seaboard fields of the Solway estuary, for instance, curlews sometimes seem to preserve a density of one to the square yard. Curlews were in company early not for the usual reason, a change in temperature, but because the land was dry, the grass was dying back and food was no longer to be had in sufficient quantity. Even the seaboard marshes were affected by drought and the sides of creeks and sandy banks were eroding, as they always do: not by the action of the ebbing and flowing water backed up by the tide, but by the warmth of the sun and the force of the occasional winds that carried away whatever clouds happened to darken the mellow autumn sky. Where did all the curlews go? I didn't keep track of them.

A friend reported large numbers of peewits on a field inland. Thousands, he said; but there may have been a hundred or two. This field is on the lower side of a water table. It is always green and wet. The peewits have gone there, perhaps finding nothing much to their liking along the coast.

If no one among my shooting acquaintances cared very much where all the curlews had gone, and wasn't interested in the place of plovers, they studied the mallard. These weren't in many of their usual places, but out on the open water of lakes in company. Mallard are gregarious in mid-winter and they keep company at all times, but no one had seen quite so many in the open as early as this. The answer was quite simple. They had nowhere else to go. A mallard doesn't care to rest in a dry ditch by day, and once the stubbles have been gleaned it flights to waterholes and ponds. The ponds had shrunk. The waterholes tended to show a cracked mud surface. If they contained any water it was away down in the black porridge across which even our springer spaniel managed to run without getting more than four black stockings for her foolhardiness. Coots and moorhens were everywhere at a greater density than normal. All at once gregariousness could be seen for what it really is; a symptom of the food shortage with a temporary intensification of competition. When the general level of water rises, as it must when the rainfall averages out, things will change. The curlews will stay on the seaboard marshes, of course. The peewits will come down from their oasis in the back country and the duck will spread themselves out and not be as numerous on the lakes again until January or February.

Fuel for Winter Fires

At the beginning of each winter we buy a load of logs. It is usually a transaction that takes place about the time the leaves turn colour and the first nip of frost is felt at dusk. The logs we get are fairly small ones, cut from the scrubby little old oak trees that have been felled in one of the valleys round about. These dwarfed trees have been growing since George Borrow walked through this countryside. The wood has the aroma that oak logs have, and when they are stacked neatly in the corner I feel we have made provision for a hard winter. We begin to use them almost at once and the neighbourhood gets that wood smoke on the breeze. Sometimes on a frosty night I step outside for a breath of cool fresh air and sniff the smoke, so much improved when one smells it out of doors. I go out because a wood fire stupefies me, while it heats the room, but I stay out only for a minute or two, and on my return I put up my feet and let my thoughts drift.

Occasionally we have company. Our visitors come in aglow with the colour of health in their cheeks. They unbutton their coats and jackets, lay aside their scarves, and say, 'Ah, oak logs.' Having said this, they gradually become less articulate. They fall silent, they seem to brood, they sigh, getting more and more flushed, less able to collect their wits, for the air in the room is devoured by the fire. Someone yawns and all find it hard to keep their eyes open. Try as we may, the conversation flounders, references become vague and allusions seem pointless. Tea is produced. What a refreshing thing is tea, but when the flames rise and the ash spreads on the hearth, tea increases a body's heat, raises the internal temperature and does nothing to clear the brain. The clock ticks drowsily on, a fragment falls into the well of the fire and the sparks dance and slowly, as the heat radiates as from a furnace, the drug does its work. The cat has long since fallen asleep. The windows are misted, the spell of the spirits of the oak glade is complete and, gently and unselfconsciously, someone snores. Time is nothing, but the slow rising and falling of the sleeper's breast and the shadow play on walls and ceiling.

Now one has friends in whose presence one can keep silent, yawn, doze and even snore, but I am the sort of person who likes to sleep unobserved, even by a bleary-eyed, cat-napping friend. When my eyelids become heavy, I think of the cool sheets and the temperate regions of the bedroom. At such times I am aware that a log fire is a sensual indulgence. It would, it seems, be a healthy thing to get out in the crisp air, to walk to the back of beyond with the wind taking my breath and the clouds sailing overhead, engulfing the stars and drowning the moon. I confess I think about it as I think about the frozen ruts of the lane on a Sunday afternoon when the robin is sitting in the leafless hedge, fluffing his feathers to conserve his warmth. I have a healthy mind. It takes me across the moor, along the wood, up to the top of the ridge to gaze into fir-lined valleys where I can see sleepy villages and white farmsteads. My body usually stays where it is. If it moves at all it goes slowly upstairs to take the refreshing contact of the bedsheets. What a destroyer of the will and the senses is a log fire!

In my childhood, although we had a log on the fire from time to time, and now and then an old moss block or bit of what is known as bog oak, the fires were of peat. Near the towns and villages there were public mosses, but in the more remote areas farmers rented a moss, a stretch of grouse moor where they acquired the right to cut peat. Peat cutting has a set of tools all its own. There are the cutters, like elongated spades, the barrows for transporting the peat to firmer ground, and the light peat carts to bring the load away from the moor. It was a summer task when the bog cotton was dancing in the wind, when the black cock called or the grasshopper sang. Sometimes in the process of cutting we encountered a moss block and managed to extricate it and sledge it across the heather, but whether we did or not, we worked in the warm sun, breathing the scent of the moor, treading the sphagnum and looking at the reflections in amber pools at the bottom of which one could see the underwater forest of weed and moss. We built the peat into little

81

pyramids, let the wind blow through them for a day or two, perhaps a week or even a fortnight if showers came, and then, when it was hard and dry, we loaded the barrows or carts and transported the peat to the hard road, beside which the alders grew and the rowans sprouted out of banks of blaeberry and the brush of heather and ling.

The harvest of peat was stacked at home and brought into the house and used as needed, four or five slabs at a time, moved in a basket and laid in the hearth. Have you ever had tea made at a peat fire or sat dreaming while peat burned? A fire of logs takes the air away and leaves a man exhausted, but a peat fire gives a soothing perfume to a room, a fragrance as subtle as that of the finest China tea. It is the very stuff of dreams. If a man has to his hand a glass of toddy and can stretch his legs to a fire of peat, he can be master of the world, king of his thoughts, lost in the wonder of his imagination and free from the hardness of life. The fireplaces of the farm were large. Sometimes the gale roared down them and sometimes hail spat in the fire, but when the storm raged the peat reek puffed out and the fine ash sailed to the ceiling and those who warmed themselves shook their heads sadly at the thought of less fortunate people walking the rough road on such a night. In this atmosphere the talk was always of fairies and demons, ghosts, and men and women who could work magic. The windows might shake and the wind whistle and moan at the door, but no one could free his mind of romantic thoughts and achieve complete unconsciousness. On such winter nights by fires of peat, the old forest of thousands of years gone, I heard the stories that came from my great-grandfather and the grandfather of my great-grandfather.

It saddens me to think that now I cannot open my door and step a yard or two for a basket of peat. We live too far from the moor and much too far from the places where peat is still cut. My children cannot know the stimulating scent that spreads as the turf begins to burn and watch the black bog slowly dissolving into powdery ash. I have no stories to tell when the oak log burns. It takes away my thought. I drift, I sigh and at times I snore.

Towards the end of winter we sometimes find we have no logs left and then the evening fire is a fire of coal. The best black, shining coal, with all the radiance while it burns, is yet not peat. It fumes, it gives a coloured flame, but the story it tells is a story of darkness and underground tunnels. All it has that reminds me of the forest and the bog is the firedamp smell, a whiff of marsh gas—the smell of ferment as long locked up in the earth as the bones of a dinosaur. When the time comes that our evening fire is a fire of coal, I am ready for spring. I am prepared to go out and look at the river and wonder about the February Red and the Hawthorn fly. I have done with dormouse dozing at night and I listen by day for the mad delight of the peewit as it flies across the low land. The fire burns brightly in spring and I think of the frost that might blight the tips of early potatoes and at times I wonder about the unfortunate man who has spent his winter by a hissing gas fire or an ugly electrical element. There is no story, no whisper of magic, nothing to stimulate the mind in the burning of gas or the white heat of a coil of wire. Oh the unhappy man who is doomed to such an existence! Oh the empty world of him who has never sprawled in a chair in a room heavy with peat reek. I almost come to weep for him. The beauty and wonder of the world has been transformed for him in a retort or a generator, a mass of steel, flashing flywheels and coiling pipes, and he is left with a fume and a hissing noise or a silent, soulless glowing thing as impersonal as only the products of man's invention can be.

Christmas Tales from the Village

There were always tales from the village when we lived there—amusing tales, scandalous tales, tales to be taken with a pinch of salt. We sifted through them, laughed at them, and did our best not to get involved in anything through repeating the wrong sort of anecdote. Characters flourished in the village in those days; of course, they have not all died just because we have left. The village is being urbanised, populated by commuters, or transformed to some extent, because many people go out each day to earn their living in distant places. The smithy is long since closed. The garages and filling stations thrive. When I go back there I think of some of the characters I used to know—worthies like Harry Chipshop, Willie Bach and Billy Brwas.

Willie Bach was famous for his minor mischiefs and the ways he employed to smooth the rough path of his life. Once he was engaged by the butcher to deliver a Christmas duck, plucked and 'oven-ready,' as the ad-men have it these days. On the way it crossed Willie's mind that, if he helped himself to some cloakroom tickets at the church hall, he could make considerably more than 6d. by running a raffle as he walked through the bar of his favourite inn. This he did, collecting perhaps 15s. or £1, and promising to deliver the prize to the winner when the requisite number of tickets had been sold. It was several days before his victims awoke to the swindle, and Willie's explanation was simple. He had drawn the ticket himself, believe it or not; but, since it was a bespoke bird, he had to forgo the prize which had, in a sense, only been borrowed. He had drunk the cash prize.

Harry Chipshop was another resourceful fellow—right on the mark when the opportunity presented itself. It was Harry's annual custom to break the law and get locked up for Christmas, so that he could enjoy the warmth and comfort of a cell as well as a good dinner or two. He generally achieved this end by doing such damage as would get him taken into custody. The policeman in the village had become a little weary of this ritual: perhaps he had been reprimanded for playing into the hands of a rogue. As hard as Harry Chipshop tried to expose himself to arrest, equally the policeman strove to turn a blind eye and ignore him.

The sergeant who looked over the constable's domain saw Harry Chipshop's pitiful condition and his heart melted. Drawing the poor, wet and bedraggled fellow on one side, he told him that he could not oblige by having him arrested, nor would he give him money for drink; but, if he liked to go to the village chipshop (whence he had derived his nickname), he could eat as much as he could at the sergeant's expense. After all, it was the season of goodwill towards all men. Harry Chipshop hurried off. He never looked a gift horse in the mouth. The owner of the chipshop quite naturally checked with the sergeant, albeit at somewhat long range. The sergeant waved and said it was all right. He would pay.

Something over three weeks later the chipshop owner managed to waylay the kindly sergeant. Would he care to settle the bill? The sergeant dug in his pocket for half-a-crown, and learned to his dismay that it was a vastly different tally. Harry Chipshop had had more than a score of large meals, all of them booked down to his benefactor. It was, after all, small compensation for three or four days in a comfortable cell, with perhaps a good helping of turkey and stuffing thrown in.

I miss this kind of tale these days; but the other evening a friend was good enough to bring me up to date with one about Billy Brwas. It has, I think, a certain compassion about it, pathos and an ironical twist that would have pleased O. Henry. Billy Brwas smiled at the world. If sadness assailed him, it was the inward sadness that belongs to the long-afflicted. When Billy amused the village and the small world that knew him, laughter was choked back. Towards Christmas one year poor Billy, an ageless boy selling newspapers to the customers of the hostelries of the village (there has since time immemorial been one inn to every nonconformist chapel in the place whether by accident or design no one can say), was depressed a little by the fact that everyone had money for presents from their Christmas clubs and draws, and he had none. There was no way that he could think of that seemed certain to bring him the money he so badly wanted, so he sat down and, slowly and painfully, composed a letter to 'Jesus in Heaven.'

'Dear Jesus,' he wrote, 'it is coming on Christmas, and I have no money to buy presents or get myself merry. Could you send me some? I know you have everything up there. Your loving Billy.' The letter was duly stamped and posted, and in the course of time found its way to the postmaster's desk, where it was opened to be returned to the sender in the usual way. The postmaster read it and was touched. He showed it to his staff, who were also deeply moved. A collection was made, and the sum of £2 was raised. It was sent to Billy Brwas in an official envelope with no accompanying explanation. No reply was expected: Billy Brwas's powers of concentration were limited. There have been many recipients of charity who have shown no gratitude, and it was known that Billy was like a grasshopper sailing on across a hayfield.

They were wrong, however. Billy made a second great effort to write a letter, and the postmaster received it in due time. He read it, expecting the gratification that even the philanthropist may enjoy. It was not a long letter. It said: 'Dear Jesus, I knew you had everything up in Heaven and you would send me money. It come allright. I expect you sent me more than two pounds, but them beggars at the Post Office opened the envelope and pinched the rest, I'm sure.'

It was not entirely the grammar or the phrasing that made the letter a great testimony of faith. Billy obviously knew the wickedness of the world and the goodness of God; but his spelling of the word beggars was wrong, profane—and wilful.

Snowed In at Christmas

It didn't happen overnight, and I remember things that led up to our being snow-bound more clearly than the day when the snow fell in earnest. I was about five years old and my impressions are those of a child fascinated by the sight of the pump beyond the kitchen window wearing a sort of overcoat with straw stuffing, the trough from which the plough horses drank brimming over in a lip of thick ice, and away beyond our march boundary, and the round hills of our neighbours' land, the Galloway hills, glazed with snow that was sometimes dazzling. Before the snow came, all sorts of precautions were taken. Swedes were piled in places where they could be easily fed to cattle, straw was put down at one of the gates, sheep were herded into the stackyard. It was only a few days until Christmas when we heard stories of trains being stuck.

I was coddled and swathed in scarves and extra woollen garments before I was taken up through the court to see how icicles had formed on the gates. The stable barrow was firmly fixed in the midden, which was as hard as iron. It was coming again, the year of the big snow, someone said. The frost was getting at potatoes in the barn and wild birds were tame, or so hungry that they could be caught without difficulty. The peat stack and the coal heap were welded, and it was necessary to break the fuel out. The milk churn lids were sticking to a man's fingers. It only needed a fall of snow, and we should be wrapped up in a blanket, cut off from the outside world.

There were snow buntings in the stackyard, and a sort of steam was rising from the shed where calves and bullocks were penned: a wall of humid air against the barrier of freezing atmosphere outside. I remember being hurried out to the door to watch the geese coming. It was long past the time for the geese to come. They had been with us for two or three months, but now a fresh wave of geese came out of the north. There was snow on the way, they said, and it was a good thing we had hams hanging, oatmeal and flour, tea and sugar by the sack. The house was always snug, but now it was made even more snug. I was examined for chapped hands and chapped legs. The embrocation bottle was brought out in case someone got the 'hoast'. My grandfather checked another bottle—the principal ingredient for the toddy made with hot water and brown sugar. As far as I was concerned, it was all exciting. My elders were worried about getting the milk out if the road happened to be closed by snow. Someone had to go away down to the bog field to bring home an old horse. I watched as they tried to pick up a stick to help them along, but the stick was fastened to the mud and the mud was as hard as the cobbles of the court, which didn't unfreeze at noon. It snowed in the night. No one told me. I looked at the skylight. Every morning I had admired the frost pictures on the glass, but now the attic bedroom was dimly lit. A covering of snow made the ceiling look yellow. It had never looked yellow before.

When I got down to the kitchen, the windows were steamed on the inside but the steam was freezing on the window ledge. The glare of snow beyond the windows stretched upwards to the sky and hills, and fields were blended with far-off higher hills and the heavens above them. It snowed all day, and late in the afternoon a path was cut across to the byre and the dairy and then another path to the stable, the cartshed and the open-sided shed where bullocks bellowed and hung their heads over the spruce poles dribbling straw on to the snow. By the next day we were cut off. It was harder to free the pump handle than it had been. Two kettles of water were needed and the water running over the spout of the pump began to turn into a stick of ice.

Everything became capped with snow. The drystone walls disappeared and indoors the few newspapers became tattered and torn, they were read so often. No one had ever had so much time on their hands before, I think. There was nothing to do but talk, drink the hot gruel that was made to warm the body up before an excursion was made to feed the standing-in beasts. The first day's milk was put in churns, the second day's supply went into spare churns and scalded butts, and then the pigs and calves began to get double rations. We had come to a crisis, it seemed, although I was hardly old enough to understand just how serious it was. Someone was sent out over the fields to make contact with the nearest cottage. The journey might have taken half an hour, but it wasn't until nightfall that word came back that everyone else was in the same predicament. The roads were closed. I forget whether anyone said that it was Christmas Eve or Christmas Day. I remember there was a serious attempt to dig a path across country so that milk might be sledged out on a hay sledge, but perhaps the creamery itself was isolated or the horsepower for such an enterprise couldn't be managed on ground that crossed covered-in burns and waterholes.

I enjoyed the company, the warmth of over-large peat fires and the feeling of being secure in a closed-in world. The snow began to melt after some days. It revealed the line of drystone dikes and black ditches, gaunt thorn trees and stunted bushes one day, and the next the road was running in slush. Someone found a ewe huddled in between a wall and the melting mound of a snowdrift. I remember being taken to see the miracle of how that sheep had survived and noticing the stained ground on which she had lain. As far as I can remember we lost no stock. The milk fattened the pigs, but of course gallons of it had to be poured away.

It seemed a lot colder when it was all over, and bleak too. The wind moaned in the porch and the porch roof leaked where the melting snow seeped in. Such a thing never happened again for me to remember it. I suppose you might say that was one Christmas we never had, for no one took note that it had come or remarked upon it until it had gone.

Some Ghosts that Died

On reflection I find that all the ghosts I might have known, from the earliest days of my childhood until now, when I am a little over the hill, have eluded me in a most frustrating way. Ghosts manifest themselves to some people and not to others, and this was true of two near-at-home ghosts I looked for every time I passed their way when I was between five and seven years of age. How I looked for them! I knew exactly where to look. I knew the sort of days when they were both likely to be seen. I had someone to warn me to be on the alert for them. I was even told in a whisper when they were there, and yet I never saw either the tinker's ghost or the stonebreaker's ghost. One sat beside the drystone wall on the edge of the moss, sheltering under a lightning-struck ash tree, if a ghost needs shelter, and the other perched on the great block of carefully built boulders he normally would have been cracking day in and day out had he lived so long.

The stonebreaker's ghost was his supernatural successor and heir to a stoneheap that was never reduced to cracked stone. He held sway there, my elders told me, until the weeds grew through the stones. All ghosts are exhibitionists of course, and like to be seen. The stonebreaker's ghost couldn't function among the long grass and the docks and thistles that eventually grew among the boulders, and he went his way after sitting there on dark winter afternoons and drowsy summer evenings alike. He must have heard the nightjar and the black cock calling, as well as the greylag geese flying away over to the river, and kept his vigil while happy cottars came home from the public house with the moon to guide them as they staggered on. He was there for long enough, and the tinker's ghost wasn't too far away from him, and he had been there much longer. I didn't see the tinker, but once, when I asked about him as the pony and trap walked the slippery hollow past his stamping ground, my grandfather assured me that he was examining a copper pot he had just soldered. Sometimes he put down his pot and smoked a clay pipe. I suppose he looked into the branches of the tree upon which one of his relations had hung a rusty horseshoe or, more likely, slung the shoe the way the ploughmen did when they used horseshoes to play quoits, making it spin round the broken branch before finally it came to rest without dropping the 30 feet or so to the road.

The tinker died too, not just for me, but as a supernatural feature of that lonely place, when traffic moved a little faster. People need time to see ghosts. Busy men and men in a hurry rarely see them. The tinker's ghost was talked about by the generation that had known him, but I doubt if anyone passing that spot now realises that once it was haunted, not only by a tinker but a stonebreaker for good measure, the ghost of a man I could remember waving to us when we passed that way going to the creamery or into the town farther on. I should like to have had a passing acquaintance with either of those two. I might even have had a genuine nostalgia for them now, but they ignored me. Some people had a way of ignoring children in those days, and both ghosts were a hangover from Victorian times. I am not belittling ghosts in any way. I could hardly do that with fey people in my ancestry, and at least one genuine witch among them, to say nothing of those with second sight.

It seems to me that country people see more ghosts than their counterparts in the town, and country mansions, rectories and castles, which are almost always out in the wilder parts of rural landscape, tend to be more persistently haunted. The house in which we lived before we came here had a 'grey' lady who revealed herself one afternoon to my wife and was never seen again. My father seemed to hover here after his death, and once I could have been persuaded that I saw him stalking down the path with the bucket he carried to feed his hens slung over his arm, but I am wary of emotional ghost-seeing. It may be wishful thinking or auto-suggestion.

That my father lingered here for a while is not confirmed, and I can't help thinking of the grey man who sat up on the hillside overlooking a remote lake which I and an old friend used to fish. The grey man was pointed out to me on a bright afternoon, and once I had seen him I looked in his direction regularly. He disappeared before the day was out. He wasn't there the next time I fished in the lake, but later on I saw him. In time I plucked up courage to go up the scree and see if we could become better acquainted. He wasn't there when I reached his seat. Later on I decided that he manifested himself when the rock was wet and the light came from a particular angle. A landslide put paid to him, I think. No one saw him after a summer of drought in which the dry earth crumbled away from the place below the rock, and finally, after the first heavy downpour, the rock itself came bowling down on to the shore. The grey man was typical of my ghosts.

When a ghost was reported in one of the outlying villages near our old home I thought I might be in at the kill there. It was a Christmas ghost of all things, and it had appeared in the street in the early hours of Christmas morning. It was in the best tradition of hauntings, clothed in white, and after standing for a long time it simply vanished. The witnesses were two elderly ladies across whose lips had never passed anything more potent than the smallest sip of cowslip wine, and that only in the far-off days of their youth. The white ghost was really covered in snow. Had it been snowing the manifestation might have been easily explained, but that year we had no snow. It was one of those mild damp Christmases that would have turned *A Christmas Carol* into a farce had it just been published. I talked to one or two people about it, but the village policeman put paid to it all so far as I was concerned, although the story persisted for at least two seasons after that. It seemed that old Harry Jones, who slept in barns and did casual work for the farmers, had hauled himself off to sleep in a shed that had been used for feathering geese for the market. The feathers had stuck to his damp, black coat, and sometime after midnight, feeling dizzy, but as thirsty as ever, Harry had tried to return to the inn. He had lost his sense of direction and his bearings after reeling in the street down by the yew tree.

The policeman, riding that way on Christmas morning, had seen the heels of him sticking out from under the tree and had extricated the poor fellow and quietly escorted him back to the station, until Boxing Day.

Ghosts are more often than not persistent. They take a lot of killing, but the majority of them rarely last three-score years and ten. The ones I have almost encountered have all proved too ephemeral for me to strike acquaintance with them.

Village News by Word-of-mouth

When my neighbour tells me that he has been away at some big agricultural event, like the Royal Show, or has been on the telephone talking to a relative in some other part of the Principality about sheep, I can't help thinking how different the world is from the one I knew as a child. Communications we had, of course, but not many farmers had motor cars and few had the telephone. The milking machine wouldn't have done very much without a generator, for electricity hadn't been slung across the shire. Ours was a small world in which gossip passed from one to another—with fantastic colour added. We knew who was giving up or going out, because we went to the places where news was exchanged—the market, the creamery, the joiner's shop and the smithy. Here we learned that a neighbour was sowing out a cornfield, or ploughing another that had long been fallow, that the tenant of such-and-such a place had cultivated a feud with the keeper, and might not get his lease renewed, and that the servant girl at so-and-so's had departed in disgrace.

The blacksmith's shop was where I learned about the world. My education may have been an earthy one, but where else could I have seen the way a burn could be made to drive a waterwheel and thereby power a lathe and a drilling machine? The smith had two sons, one with bright red hair and the other with black. They were always at odds, and once I went home in horror to tell how they shaped up to each other with coal shovels, about to emulate Cain and Abel. The red-haired smith taught me to fish for trout. We cooked them on the shovel, which was suitably burnished for the job. But what was a small child doing there? I would be sent with 'a line' to the smith, warning him of the need to be ready to shoe the ploughing team before the start of a new week, or of some urgent repair required on a binder or reaper.

I always stayed as long as I could. I gathered news and brought it home. Not very important news for the most part, but a contribution to the communications link. 'Tell your grandfather,' the smith would say, 'that Mr McKenna will be putting his sheep through the dip on Tuesday, in case he doesn't know.' It was information of this kind that saved a lot of walking to find out when sheep were being dipped. Our sheep were dipped with Mr McKenna's. There was no telephone by means of which we could have had the information—in a minute, and for a penny.

At the creamery of a morning we would sometimes queue to unload our milk churns, waiting perhaps a quarter of an hour for the milk to be tested and poured into the vat, and new churns pushed out to us across the loading platform. Talk ranged over almost everything under the sun: the kind of foal the brood mare had had, the price of oilcake and why the seed merchant's traveller was late upon his rounds. Sometimes a neighbour with whom we shared a march wall would tell us that rebuilding was needed. A bull had toppled the stones. We were asked for the use of a hay sweep, or told how the daughter of that particular family had won a bursary to Edinburgh. When there was no longer an excuse for dallying we turned the horse and jangled off home, trying to get our priorities right, and keeping in mind the important items of the news we had gathered. We gathered a little more on the way, for we noted that so-and-so was already carting hay, or that the crows had been on his potatoes, or the rooks had pulled his swedes.

The postman was the most important bearer of news in the whole district. He would be all day about his task of delivering letters, catalogues and gossip, to say nothing of important messages to a host of people who didn't see one another from market day to market day. The post brought yesterday's newspaper. Ailing kings and sick politicians died 24 hours before we knew of their departure, but all was relative, and a state funeral was none the worse for being a day behindhand. Death is the only certain thing in life. Perhaps because of this the postman lingered if ever we received a black-edged envelope. No doubt he had already shown the symbol of death and bereavement to people along the way and they would want to know, on the following day, what relative we had in London or Glasgow. In such a community the bell tolls for one and all, faint thought it may sound when two or three hundred miles separate them from their kin.

The red face of the postman reminded me of the red skins of apples we dipped for at Hallowe'en. It seems to me now that he was more often sitting at our table prodding bread-crust into the yolk of a newly-topped egg than riding his mailbag-hung bicycle. But then the postman was a close friend, almost a relative. He certainly lived close to every family he called upon. He knew their grief and their delight. He also knew when they were in debt, of course, and where an estranged son or daughter had gone to live the moment they wrote home. He had no need to steam open the mail or hold a flimsy letter to the light to read its message. He would drink tea and listen to the news being read aloud, shaking his head and clicking his tongue. There was no way to curb such curiosity. To conceal the contents of a letter was to invite speculation.

There was one other link in the network of human contact that few people dared ignore: the cattle show. For here all that had passed in a year of word-of-mouth could be confirmed. Relatives, friends and second-cousins, great-uncles and great-aunts, searched for one another and looked into faces that had known loss or sickness.

This world goes faster now. There is no denying that. A day's travel is no longer what a man may walk or ride, the range of a pony pulling a gig or what a brass-lamped, heater-less, prone-to-boiling car might journey at a reckless 30 to 40 miles an hour. We get our news before it happens. Its impact barely stimulates our long-dulled reflexes. Oh for the day when my eyes grew large and my mouth fell open to hear of a pony rearing at a traction engine, and tipping passengers and driver into the ditch! Oh for the day when the trees were twice as tall, and we had time to stand on the road and talk and speculate about the sound of hoofbeats or the grinding of wheels on some far-away hill!

Country Characters

A Man Apart, a Role Unchanged

The Moorland Shepherd

We weren't so far from the moor when I was a boy, and one way and another I got to know the moorland shepherd, who was quite a different sort of man to the farm herd, the man who looked after a flock on the pasture. For one thing, the moorland shepherd was his own master. He lived out there, remote from other people, with his family and his dogs. He was a sort of Robinson Crusoe in the matter of being self-sufficient. He was shy of people, redder of face than even the ploughman who butted into the rain and the wind as he held the plough and talked to his team on a winter's day.

When he came into the town it was usually for the mart, the sheep sales. He generally brought one or two dogs with him as well as his wife and a child in arms. He often lost sight of his wife and the baby in the course of the day, but he was never without his dogs. They either cowered nervously at heel when he was taking a dram—and he took so many sometimes that he swayed on his feet—or waited outside for him, snarling at the curs of the town and savaging them when they became too bold. When the occasion was over the shepherd and his family went off back into the moor, vanishing in the dusk like the bird flying into the night. They were forgotten until they came down again for 'messages', items of groceries essential to life out there in the blue haze where nothing moved, except sheep, and the grouse flying from one peat shoulder to the next.

No American Indian was more of an enigma to the townsman. The moorland dweller was the son and the great-grandson of generations of solitaries, men who had kept flocks away back in biblical times, I always felt. Their eyes were full of wonder, and they were stimulated on those few occasions when they appeared on the streets of the town, loping rather than walking, I always thought, and looking farther ahead than ordinary men because they were used to bigger horizons. When they went home they weren't daunted by the seeming endlessness of the moorland roads, the forests of bracken, the high, lichened drystone walls they passed through, the shadows of gorse and bog myrtle tossed in the wind. They were used to that kind of world. Had they been afraid of the dark they would never have survived.

Except when they were drunk they were quiet men, not given to raising their voices. If they did, it was to command a dog, although most commands were conveyed by whistles. Even their dogs didn't bark at the town dogs as they left, but growled and bared their fangs.

Moor farms were hardly farms but huddles of stone with buttressed gables leaning out of stone folds, and roofs that were green with algae if they were slated, tufted with growing grass when they were sod-covered. Invariably there was a reek of peat being burned, and the cackle of a hen or two. The growing brood of children peered shyly from behind the bush or the peat stack. The background was a vast wilderness, rolling moor, rising, cloud-dappled hills, all of it awe-inspiring to a person used to the town because it could have been the surface of the moon but for the bleating of sheep. The sheep were always shaggy blackfaces, and the old rams with their curls of horn had almost human expressions. Lambs dotted the whole landscape in early summer. The shepherd was never at home, but somewhere out there where the curlew called.

The living was never good. It was not a living but a way of living close to poverty, but the thing the shepherd knew by instinct, the only thing he could, or would, think of doing. The limit of his social contact with men was the sheep sale and those days when he joined a neighbour to share the task of shearing or dipping the flocks. Dipping would be done on some moorland burn where a sluice had been constructed and sheep could be driven from fold to fold and through bottle-necked pens to the dip. Shearing was done by hand, and the shearers made the most of the occasion to talk sheep, crack jokes, eat and drink.

We used to have a sheep dog trained by these moorland shepherds. There was nothing they didn't know about breaking in a young dog, and when the thing was done they were careful to remind the dog's owner that it had been taught to do things in a certain way. It must be worked that way, never thrashed for disobeying, never shouted at. The implication was that the dog couldn't be a fool but its owner was most likely one, which was often the case! The moorland dog could control a flock of sheep by pricking his ears or gently switching his tail from one side of his body to the other. Its way with sheep would give any layman a feeling of inferiority and make him selfconscious when he gave a command.

There has been change on the moors as there has been everywhere. The moorland shepherd trundles down to the mart in a battered Land-Rover these days. He has the same dogs, walks the same miles over the peat hags, and lives in the same huddle of stones. But the sheep are shorn with electric shears now. Up on the moor the heather has given place to a useless grass in many places. There are far fewer grouse packs or blackcock to perch on the dead thorn and keep a lookout. The silence is much the same. No one can change the shape of the wild hills. No one carts away the stone walls or diverts the water. For a while they poisoned the sheep's parasites with dieldrin in the dip. The wash-out killed a lot of insects, and there are now fewer insectivorous birds in these places, but in the main there is no significant change in this ancient way of life.

Fortunately a man can't lamb a flock from a helicopter, even if deer have been shot from one. There is no other way but the hard old way, which is no harder on the moorland shepherd than it has ever been.

The Old Poacher

The last of the 'old poachers' of my early recollections died in the 1950s. I remember going to see him when I was on a visit to the part of the world in which I spent my childhood and early boyhood, making the mistake of trying to recapture something of what had been a wonderful world. He was a ploughman in the days of horse-ploughing, and not a bad hand when it came to ploughing matches, but his proper description was that of being 'an old poacher'. Unlike the people of Wales, who are inclined to use the word old as a term of affection for anyone crossing swords with authority, old when applied to a poacher meant quite simply that he was incurable. His addiction was as firmly fixed as that of the man who loitered on the step of the public house first thing in the morning. A dog was called an old poacher, and shot, and the laird's keeper would have done this to Jeck had he thought he could have done so with impunity.

The old keeper lived away back in the early 19th century, in a world in which the mantrap and deportation were mentioned in the same breath. If he had had his way, Jeck, who worked for my grandfather for a number of years, would have found a new horizon in which to snare rabbits under the Southern Cross, and pit his wits against the kangaroo. I dare say he would have done this with great success, but he and the laird's man never came into confrontation as principal witness and accused.

Jeck's fieldcraft was unsurpassed and on reflection I think it was because he was an amateur. He didn't poach for money. He was obsessed by the challenge of the business, which was to catch anything that used a track or dropped down to a particular patch of ground more than once. The keeper's patrol, the threat of being taken 'with coneys', as the charge might have read, simply made the whole thing more satisfying when it came off. And it hardly ever failed to come off, for Jeck had the mind of a snarer and a fowler. Whenever I heard that particular part of the scripture that mentioned the fowler's snare Jeck immediately came to mind. His face was more familiar to me than the face of Samson or John the Baptist.

If I worshipped Jeck it was because he treated me like a man. He explained things so clearly that I had no difficulty in setting snares in the right places, or deciding when the gate net would be ineffective. It sometimes was, because sound or scent would be carried down wind and then anything out in the darkness of the field would simply circle and go on circling in front of the dog.

I became Jeck's apprentice when I was allowed to stay out in the stable while everyone else cleared up after the milking. Jeck, in his capacity of ploughman, didn't milk. His concern was his team, which he fed and groomed and kept company with until it was time to go in for his supper. On these occasions Jeck worked away fashioning snares, sorting his nets and other bits and bobs of poaching equipment which he kept stowed away in a harness cupboard. He would sit on the corn chest with the storm lantern beside him and deftly fashion nets, or make ready bunches of snares which he would use over the next few days. He could snare anything from a rat, or even a mole, to a pheasant or a hare. He didn't go in for rabbit snaring very much except when he wanted to demonstrate that he could catch a particular rabbit that ran over a particular knowe or knoll as he led his horses in from the grass. He wired for pheasants and took them on their tracks through the fence, and sometimes through the hedge or the brush leading to places where the keeper was in the habit of feeding.

The deftness of his fingers always fascinated me. He could make a loop and turn it into a hitch or draw it into the mesh of a net with what was almost sleight of hand. He caught things the same way, and if he saw a rat scurrying along the bottom of the drystone wall of the rickyard he didn't make a hullaballoo and shout for the dog, but watched quietly and shortly afterwards set a snare and caught the creature. In his collection of gear he had fine nets and heavy nets, and in the making of them time was unimportant. He didn't seem to concern himself with how long it took but only with the making of a good net.

I remember him making the net which was used at my initiation into the secrets of catching things at the fivebar gate, and the night we left the lantern burning at the stable window while we went out to see what the dog could bring to us. The dog was borrowed from a cottager neighbour who had 'never done a hand's turn' of work in his life, according to my aunts. He and Jeck sometimes went long-netting together, but not on any regular basis because Jeck didn't care about the rewards and wouldn't 'do' a place more than once, being convinced that this was the certain way to 'jile'.

There was no kind of snare I wasn't taught to set up, and if I had to I think I could still do so, but what I found most exciting was gate netting. Jeck always knew when the wind was right for a particular situation and of course he had always made a round of the field to stop escape routes with bits of blackthorn or whin, for this was essential if the game on the field was to come to the gate and the net. On that first occasion we only got a hare. A second setting immediately after we had taken the hare failed to take anything. It was a bad night for the switchback hill, Jeck said. The dog had ranged too far out and then circled after hares that had probably heard us scrambling to take the first as it struggled in our net.

This particular operation wasn't really poaching. We were at home, but it was only a step after that, to cross the march dike and go deeper into pastures if not new, less familiar to me, until one day I found myself

101

pounding up through a wood with the keeper not far behind. He put the fear of death in me, firing a shot into the branches of the larches. The falling debris struck my neck and I thought I was shot! Jeck the 'old poacher' gave me a lecture about that. I had taken a wrong turning. Venturing close to the rearing pens made me not much better than a turkey thief. Where was the art in catching tame birds? I could catch our own farmyard hens with a chaff riddle.

Jeck hardly ever used a gun, except when he took one along when he went to plough. But he was a great hand with a throwing stick. I once saw him bring down a cock pheasant from the top of a rick by throwing a hammer at it. No one I ever encountered could look at ground and sum up what it might hold, and where the game would lie, better than Jeck. It was an instinct only a throw-back could possess, and I am sure that the laird, who was a fine old sporting gentleman would have found something in Jeck despite his infamous reputation. They might even have come to terms about the whole thing. Respectability can become tarnished however and even a boy's reputation had to be nurtured. I suppose that was why Jeck moved on. No one said that he was a bad influence but a neighbouring farmer had become rather outspoken about my excursions over her land when I hadn't as much as set foot on her side of the wall. I lost touch with my 'master' and gradually my good name was restored.

On that sentimental journey back to Galloway I was in the village in which Jeck had been born and bred when I heard that he was still alive, though sorely stricken. I went to see him and asked him if he 'had mind of me'. He lifted his head from his pillow and smiled. Yes, he had mind of the scratching I had suffered lifting a hare from the snare, and he had mind of me diving at the gate net to grab, not a hare, but the spitting fury of a wild farm cat which the lurcher had started from the field. They had been great days and he hoped I hadn't forgotten the things he had shown me for he hadn't shown them to anyone else. Jeck's wife ushered me out, shaking her head sadly. 'He minds you, and you will mind him. Many's the pheasant he took,' she said. I couldn't help smiling at the understatement.

The Stonebreaker as Idol

Like every small child, I longed to grow up and be whichever of my elders happened to be my temporary idol. There were days when I wanted to be the driver of the threshing 'mill' that travelled about the countryside making a train of the great engine with its smoking stack, the threshing machine and the living quarters of the threshing team pulled at the back like the guard's van on a proper train. I wanted to count my sheep on the hill, be a groom and lead a stallion all braided and brushed to perfection or to be a keeper and walk the fields with three or four fine liver spaniels.

I also for a time wanted to be a stonebreaker. On reflection I can't think what took my imagination there, for there was surely no more sedentary occupation than this one. The stonebreaker sat next to a great mountain of boulders or quarried rock, cracking the larger lumps into pieces suitable for the roadmender. The roadmender was just a carter who loaded the cracked rocks and plodded along, leading his horse until he came to the first pothole. He filled it as best he could and plodded on to the next one.

I suppose he took all day or even several days to use a cartload because the stonebreaker didn't work overtime. He sat there looking out at the 'forest moor' on one side, and the green hills of a dairy farm on the other. He brought his dinner with him, and although I know I must have jogged past him many times when it was raining, I cherish the illusion that the quarry was always bathed in sunshine and the leaves on the rowan trees were always fluttering in the soft breeze of the morning.

A bird always sang in a hawthorn tree on the bank above the quarry, which was open to the road and not very big. Most of the stones piled there had been carted so that they could be broken. The original rock mound, not a very high one, had been exhausted, although enough of it remained to keep the place sheltered and a sort of suntrap, adorned along its far end by tall gorse. It was always summer there. The gorse was a wonderful contrast of strong green and butter gold, and a long-tailed tit nested in it, for I had explored it with the stonebreaker one day while my grandfather waited for me to be shown the nest. On the way back the old fellow opened his dinner box and gave me a buttered oatcake. Being always ravenously hungry, I wolfed it down, but I can remember the salty taste of it yet and wish that I could come upon such oatcakes again.

He was an old man, that stonebreaker, for my grandfather said he couldn't remember him looking any different when he himself had first come through that countryside as a youth. He had always broken stones there and everyone who passed gave him the time of day and waved to him. He always waved back, and I suppose when he heard the sound of a pony and trap on the road or someone creaking along on a ramshackle bicycle he put down his hammer and got ready to wave. I suppose, too, that he speculated what errand the passers-by were bent upon or where they had been when he saw them on the return journey. The roads were little used, of course. The traffic was sporadic, a little more on a market day, the regular passing of carts taking milk down to the creamery in the morning, or someone herding a few cattle from one place to another. Once I saw the stonebreaker sitting in the midst of a milling flock of sheep headed off at a road junction by two collies waiting for the shepherd to catch them up and indicate where he wanted the sheep to go.

That kind of world had a magic I can't properly convey. The peace, if that is the right word for it, seemed to hold things in suspension. The stonebreaker was there in the middle of it, making his tea from a small fire among smoke-blackened stones, smoking his clay pipe contemplatively, splitting stones with deft blows of the hammer which he carried home on his back at night the way a man carries a gun after an expedition over the moss or the marsh. For a long time the old fellow had sat alone, but then he all at once had a companion, a brown and white terrier that sat with him. Long afterwards I learned that the old man's wife had died and there was nothing else for it but to bring the dog with him. It couldn't be kept shut up in a cottage, and if it ran loose the keeper would shoot it.

One day it was racing up and down the quiet road as my grandfather came jogging home from town. He slowed the trap and called it, though it refused to respond. At the quarry the trap was drawn in so that grandfather could tell the old stonebreaker that his dog was demented, but the reason for the dog's strange behaviour was soon apparent. The old fellow had died, sitting there with his hammer in his hands, rock dust on his boots, his clay pipe laid to one side, and his dinner can unopened. He wasn't replaced. The loads of boulders ceased to be delivered. Instead they poured in crushed rock. Soon Tarmac equipment fouled the sweet-scented air, and the hawthorn tree lost its leaves. It, too, was very old. I was very young. My ambition to be a stonebreaker and sit watching the world go quietly by was never realised.

The Legend of Little Turpin

There isn't a shred of evidence to suggest that John Jones, police-record alias Little Turpin, alias Coch Bach y Bala (the little red one of Bala, Merionethshire), ever owned a horse, or even stole one to play highwayman. There is nothing to suggest that he robbed the rich to help any but the poor (first person singular) in a self-indulgent way. He was not a latterday Robin Hood any more than the Great Train Robbers were the legitimate heirs of the merry men of Sherwood.

Nevertheless, Coch Bach made himself a legend, although not in the mould of Robin Hood or anyone quite so respectable as that other folk hero, Twm Shon Catti. Twm Shon, considered outside the realms of Welsh fancy, was not a proper outlaw. Coch Bach lived outside the law—'Little Turpin' was an English dubbing. He had no horse and the words 'Stand and deliver!' never passed his lips. He was a petty thief all his life and it is said his individual crimes never brought him more than £3 a time.

His legend was built on the fact that he was credited with having escaped from almost every prison in which he was confined. It is also said that he spent two-thirds of his life in gaol.

Coch Bach was publicly flogged for theft in 1858, when he was six years old. He never stopped stealing things for more than fifty years after that—a duck, piglets, cutlery from the White Lion, anything and everything his hand might alight upon. And he was not even a skilled thief. Fagin would have turned him away. Charlie Peace would have scorned his work. He was caught, again and again, and it was this that led to the legend of his gift for escaping from prison.

He was blamed for every crime committed within walking distance of his native place, and he was a compulsive thief. Other thieves were happy to think that the local police put most things down to Little Turpin. When they put him away he was soon out again—and back in again, and out again! The only times the victims, police and culprits scratched their heads about giving a dog a bad name was when Coch Bach was, to use a modern police expression, 'banged up' in the local gaol, sewing mailbags or picking oakum.

The science of finger-printing came too late to save Coch Bach. He had no *modus operandi* but, much more damning, he had no alibi, and if he hadn't poached here he had poached there. If he hadn't stolen a tankard and some spoons from one particular hostelry he had taken the same sort of things from another. He was not, however, within a coach journey of being a Turpin, more of a magpie, and by no stretch of imagination a Robin Hood. Why is he held in his native place among the local boys who made good or bad? Why were the James Brothers of America held in esteem? Because they represented the have-nots, 'us' in the battle against 'them'.

Coch Bach couldn't make it now. He was a character from the age of characters and he died in a manner somewhat similar to that of many a Wild West outlaw. He was shot while on the run, and wearing his long-johns at that. His legend has more solid fact about it than even the legend of Jesse James. His death certificate bears witness. John Jones, alias Little Turpin, alias Coch Bach y Bala (every word is there on the official record) died of 'shock followed by haemorrhage, the result of gunshot wound by Reginald Jones Bateman'. The 'outlaw' was killed at Coppy Wood near Natchsyd Farm on October 6, 1913. Coch Bach was unarmed at the time but was wearing a few sacks over his long-johns, and when he made a movement that seemed to suggest he was about to draw a gun, he was shot.

Poor Coch Bach had escaped from prison at Ruthin, making a rope of his bedsheets and using it, as many another prisoner had done, to get down the wall of the castle onto a haystack. After five days on the run he encountered Mr Bateman, who was shooting partridges near Coppy Wood. Mr Bateman, to give him his due, tried hard to persuade Coch

Bach to give himself up. Coch Bach was in a wretched condition, and not at all himself, but he had no intention of surrendering. When he made his move, he was shot. The discharge from Mr Bateman's gun unfortunately severed the femoral artery in Coch Bach's right leg. In five minutes Coch Bach was dead.

At the inquest the coroner thought to ask at what stage in the apprehension of a convict such a thing could justifiably happen. The Governor of Coch Bach's prison said rather enigmatically that it depended on circumstances. One might have thought that in the circumstances the death certificate might have recorded misadventure, but it did not. It testified to the sad fact that Coch Bach, 61 years of age, occupation labourer, died as a convict who had committed breach of prison at Ruthin. Coch Bach was buried three days later.

It should be recorded that the unfortunate young man who unintentionally brought about the death of a folk hero didn't survive him for very long.

Such a thing couldn't happen nowadays. No petty thief would ever be flogged in public at the age of six, and no modern thief can become immortal by stealing piglets, hens, ducks and cutlery and escaping from a remand home. Our criminals have to do better than that, for ours is the age of big is best. We pass over Little Turpins or Coch Bachs, rarely send them to prison, and never, or hardly ever, shoot them on the run.

Men Who Moved a Mountain

There are almost as many Will Parrys in Wales as there are Bob Roberts, I have often thought, although both fall short when it comes to a headcount of the John Joneses. Will was a quarryman born and bred to working in the limestone crater his father and grandfather had helped to excavate. He had never had a hope of a comfortable retirement. A man never strikes it rich in limestone, and in the old days there was always a lot of rubbish to be trammed away before the good stuff came down to the crusher perched above the jetty. There was no money for rubbish, but it had to be moved to get at the limestone that crumbled after blasting and slithered down into the vast hole as the dust cloud rose above.

Will came to help his father and learn the trade, such as it was. He pushed trams. He man-handled lumps of rock. He made the tea, and his saliva, he told me, was a solution of limestone dust, for he breathed it in. Away up on the sun-bleached ledges seagulls nested in early May, and he often went to rob them and the rock pigeons and feral pigeons that still haunted the crags even when explosions took place day after day. It was the very hardest sort of life, and the quarry-owners would have no hesitation in sending everyone home when rain sheeted down and the sea vanished in the deluge, because they simply couldn't afford to keep men standing about when a shot couldn't be fired. The old way was hand-drilling with a jumper, Will told me, one man striking and the other turning the 'drill', which was not unlike a short crowbar.

They were hard men, these drillers and shot-firers, and very particular about the fettling of the jumper, and the making of the hammer-shaft, which was unlike the shaft of an ordinary hammer because it was resilient. It didn't transmit a shock to the man using it because it was comparatively long and fashioned from a hazel rod carefully smoothed with a broken bottle or glass jam jar.

The hammer man would go off on a Sunday afternoon in late autumn (when the wood wasn't sappy) to find the perfect hazel plant for his hammer-shaft. He would meticulously skin or bark it and shape the hazel to the hammer-head so that the implement would balance perfectly in his hands. The skill of it all depended on this selection of the stick and its preparation. A man who couldn't put a good shaft in his hammer suffered as a result, was fatigued quicker—and earned less money in the end because they were all paid as a gang on output.

In the end, of course, all that changed, and Will graduated to pneumatics. The pneumatic drill danced its way into the limestone in no time at all. Shot-firing rattled the windows in Will's village more regularly, and the rockfall was engineered at the end of the shift without difficulty. Everyone 'knocked off' knowing that tomorrow there would be work to do, providing too much rubbish hadn't been blasted down from the receding cliff face, and the trams could be hurried to and fro to feed the maw of the crusher. Occasionally someone was caught napping at the firing and was maimed for life, or even killed by the eruption of large lumps of red-grey limestone. Sometimes a tram ran over a man's foot and lamed him, or even took a foot off, but there had always been hazards of one kind or another in the quarry.

It even happened when the trams were done away with and a conveyor belt took their place. There was always someone who was unlucky and got caught up in machinery. The crusher didn't discriminate between a man and a rock, the workers soon discovered.

The boats still came in with the tide and carted the crushed limestone away for processing, but the old kilns that had nestled in minor quarries near the village became overgrown with elderberries and thorns, and no longer sheltered the itinerant tramps who sometimes crawled into them for warmth. The brow of the hill became steeper. The wind cut across the slope more keenly. The sheep that had looked safely into the abyss in the old days had to be fenced off to stop them plunging into a hole that matched the minister's description of hell's mouth when the crushers rumbled and rattled and shot after shot sent powder smoke and dust into the air.

Will gave it up in the end. His back troubled him. He began to find the constant noise more than he could stand. He also began to enjoy the beer and his bed rather more than he had done as a young man. The labour force was diminishing in any case, and the quarry finally closed. Whatever walls had been built with the massive stone, or mortar made with the crushed product, this enterprise hadn't changed the architecture of the village one whit. What a hundred years of quarrying had done was alter the headland. Generations of quarrymen had moved a minor mountain, mostly with their bare hands and a few detonators and some explosive. The crusher and the conveyor had speeded it up to finish it all off.

Will would tell the youngsters he used to work in the quarry, but they didn't really know what he was talking about when the quarry was just a hole with a kind of a milky lake at the bottom of it and some old rusty ironwork on its shore. There wasn't even an echo of the activity that had once filled the air, and the youngsters didn't know what a jumper was.

Two of a Kind

They were brothers and they were alike in appearance to an extent that made me sometimes think that they were twins. They were tall, thin and bony. They walked with the same stride and sometimes one had to look twice to be quite sure of identifying them one from the other, but they were never together. They followed the same occupation. They had no visible means of support. One was called Snib and the other Minister. Very occasionally a farmer might delude himself and think he might get a day's work out of Snib, or give the poor fellow a job that he knew wouldn't get done just to let him have a square meal. It wasn't that Snib was hurt by the offer of charity, but there was no getting rid of him when he decided he had a soft mark. He could be put off when he was reproached with the fact that only last week he had undertaken to clean out an old henhouse or piggery, and hadn't moved a barrowload, though he had filled his belly two or three times. Snib would stalk away mumbling curses which, as he put more distance between himself and the person he had taken a spite against, would rise and become a tirade of shouting.

He wore an old army greatcoat, and he had been known to come to attention and stand in that position, without explanation, for as long as a quarter of an hour. It was the greatcoat and his immobility that gave rise to the legend that he had been in the Scots Guards, but I am sure the illustrious Brigade would never have owned him. His greatcoat had lost its buttons. It was tied at the waist with twine. No guardsman taking to the road and living in old stone quarries or farm outbuildings would have lost his buttons, or even allowed them to become tarnished, for that matter.

Snib came to us one harvest. He wasn't 'waged' like the rest of the harvesters, or contracted like the men who came over the water from Ulster, but paid by the day. He was always the longest getting from the steading to the field of operations, though he had the best stride. It was his interest in things like a waterhen in the ditch, a yellowhammer on the tree, or a young rabbit popping in and out of a gorse clump that slowed him down. Then, when he was ready for work, he had a problem. His bowels were uncertain. We lost him in the farthest clump of bracken —his modesty insisted upon his going as far as he could go. He would get thirsty, or become preoccupied with a 'thistle' in his finger, and would stop in his tracks at the sight of someone coming across the open pasture carrying the tea basket. He was always the first to sit down. He ate like a hungry wolf and, although he had nowhere to go, he pestered anyone who possessed a watch to know the precise hour of the day. He didn't stay very long and he wasn't greatly missed when he went, taking his bundle on his back and putting on his greatcoat despite the heat of the August afternoon. He asked for his money. There was enough for tobacco and beer. He turned the coins in his palm, looked hard at them and spat on them before he slipped them into his pocket.

'Right you are then, sir!' he said, and stepped out at a fine pace. The distractions he had found on the way to the harvest field morning and afternoon were no longer there. He covered the ground like a loping hound and we saw no more of him for a long time. When we did encounter him he gave us a wave, frowning if we didn't show enthusiasm at the sight of him. His face was always a bristle. He hardly ever shaved although he didn't grow a beard. His hair was black and his brows were formidably bushy. We generally distinguished him from Minister by the army greatcoat.

Minister was a different character. He never compromised. He worked for no one. His temper was highly uncertain. He ranted and raved in the village street, and no one ever discovered what these fits were about. He was not a man to cross, although physically he would have been no match for a well-nourished labourer. One of his treasured possessions was a bible. He read it aloud, or perhaps he recited what he thought was scripture and couldn't read. The words were almost unintelligible, but they were reminiscent of the Old Testament rather than the New, and full of hell and damnation. When I was very small he frightened me. My heart thumped when we passed him in the gig. He never gave anyone his direct attention but cursed and harangued as though addressing a third party. No one replied or gave the slightest sign that they heard or cared about a single word. This perhaps added to his fury, although it was well-known that to react brought out the worst in Minister and he was away, like some sort of mad John Knox.

People knew him everywhere he went. He must have been aware of the effect he had upon villagers and the inhabitants of the 'wee clachans' he loved to stalk through. Women would hurry indoors and peep from the corners of windows as he passed by. Children ran, and sometimes ganged up when they had enough distance between themselves and the gaunt figure in the battered hat and dirty raincoat, shouting scorn and insults after him. This was fatal. He would stand stock still in the street and begin cursing for all he was worth. Dogs would walk warily round him, sniffing at his earthy clothes, and he would kick out at them.

I suppose the police had been on his heels a thousand times, but he was never 'taken up' as far as I knew. Unlike his brother Snib, he managed to keep comparatively clean-shaven, but his appearance was often that of a black-bearded man for he had a false beard which he put on from time to time. I think it must have had some religious significance for him. Perhaps he thought of himself as the reincarnation of John the Baptist.

The beard was made of sheep's wool and he tied it on, I remember my aunt saying. She had witnessed him changing his personality one day when she was coming out of the village shop, for there he sat on a low wall with his back to her, fishing this black sheep's wool beard from his pocket and fixing it in place. He glared at her as she went past to get on her bicycle. Not everyone had seen him put on his beard and when he put it on, he was in the habit of wearing it and never being seen without it for weeks on end so that some people who didn't know him too well thought he had grown it.

I never 'knew the going' of either Snib or Minister. They may have died in an institution, but it is more likely that they faded away, breathing their last breath in a barn or bothy, with no one to smudge their eyelids or sigh at their passing.

Paid to Grieve

Some people may find it hard to believe that there ever were professional mourners, people dedicated, one might say, to the graveyard and the ritual of burial. The profession was never one with a great future in it, although it was not unknown in Wales.

I cherish the thought that I may have watched the last practitioners of the art of mourning performing their necessary, and highly respectable office. I am not without respect for ritual myself. In Lancashire it was the thing to be properly buried 'with ham'. Farther north the wee dram was the rule. In Wales, with stronger Baptist influence perhaps, the thing that might leave a sole survivor of a family a social oddity, and a kind of untouchable, was not to have enough people around to mourn the dead. Mere spectators wouldn't do.

The village, when we first came to live in it, had begun to suffer from the erosion of its close-knit relationships. There was still a kind of Mafia one had to be careful about when second cousins, out on the lesser limbs of the family tree, were talked about. If one subscribed to hearsay, and one risked social ostracism by not doing so, all things might be revealed and inner mysteries explained.

I knew Evans the Death. He was a very fine craftsman in wood and made me a present of a slab of Japanese oak when I took up woodcarving. He was, of course, the village undertaker, but although we were on the friendliest of terms he never gave a yes or a no on whether the Joneses of the lower village were *paid* mourners. I suppose it would have been unethical. Such a revelation out of the horse's mouth would have been a breach of professional standards.

Given the bits of information I had, I had reason to believe that the Jones family (this was not their real name) were professionals.

They certainly attended a lot of funerals in dark clothing. They dallied at the graveside. They formed their own little group on the pavement when the minister held a short service at the cottage door. With no obvious link between them and a lot of deceased persons, they had to be professionals. I place some reliance on the fact that village credulity, from which the legend sprang, is a more positive factor than Bible truth. No one risks being an outcast by disputing what everyone knows.

While they said that anything was possible among people from the lower village, that very small area of two-up and two-down houses along the side of the stream, people down there were particularly human. It was not their fault that it was in flood, carrying bobbing swedes to the sea and trundling along other, less buoyant articles, like chipped enamelled buckets and the occasional unusual item such as a bassinet from Victoria's reign. The Joneses from down there were almost certainly paid to make up numbers when someone, with perhaps only a single son or daughter to mourn them, was laid to rest.

Who paid them and who had seen money change hands? There were two schools of thought. One was that Evans the Death paid them on behalf of the bereaved, and the other was that the principal mourner slipped something into the hand of their representative when he thanked them for coming. One couldn't argue against such plausible explanations. There had been five of them, father and mother and three children, two boys and a girl, but only four were there in my time. They were not impressive looking. They had pale, unhealthy complexions, but this, and their shabby respectability, gave them a certain credibility. They looked the part and capable of sharing grief in the face of death. I noticed that they were often on their way to or from the cemetery up the road from where we lived.

They were devoted to the graveyard—father who was rickety and the grimmest of them all, mother who often carried a few flowers, and the daughter, who perhaps hadn't the same talent, but had her mother's gaunt features and always clutched a black handbag as though full of remorse and sadness. The son was really a make-weight, I think, and less alert to the fact that when the bell tolled it tolled for him. None of them was particularly concerned about which denomination tolled the bell, however, non-conformist or Church of England in Wales. The wag who told me most about them said that floral tributes they sometimes brought to a funeral had been freshly gathered from a grave of yesterday. Sadly missed they would be, he told me, when they themselves went.

I shall never know if money passed, and Jenny Jones, Jenny the Grief my informant called her, gave up when her husband died. There were mitigating circumstances. The son had taken up with a woman and

113

moved away. Two professional mourners hardly make a funeral any more than two swallows make a summer. I like to think, however, that it was unbearable personal grief that made Jenny forsake the graveyard. She could, after all, have recruited a couple of relatives to stand in and make up numbers. I didn't myself see the going of her, or who might have been there to perform for her the office she had performed for so many gone before. It is twenty years since I lived in the village and longer than that since I last saw Jenny. She must certainly be gone by now.

Come to think of it, it is not unlike having seen the last bustard on Salisbury Plain, or having known the last man to shoe an ox in Wales, which I did.

Old Frank's Pony Express

The creature that pulled Old Frank along the road in the gig he bought after his light, high-wheeled one was wrecked, was the most docile of ponies—if, indeed, it could properly be called a pony, for it was a rig and somewhere between a cob and a draught horse.

Old Frank had resigned himself to being pulled by a slow, round-bellied, never-bat-an-eyelid kind of animal that brought him home from market, blind drunk, lying in the bottom of the gig without a rein within reach of either hand. It hadn't always been like that. When I was about 10 years old it was Old Frank's ambition to be a front-runner in the weekly race home from market. He saw himself passing the whole field, his pony's mane trailing in the wind and his tall wheels showering grit onto the verges. He kept this ambition secret until a couple of dealers came to him with a rangy, mean-eyed pony they said was the fastest thing on four legs—for a man who could handle it.

Frank, a very old friend of the family, persuaded them to leave the nag with him for a week, and then brought it round to have it vetted. Our horse-dealer relative, whose reputation was unsurpassed as a judge of horseflesh, was summoned to give his verdict. There was only one thing wrong with the pony, he said. It had been so abused in its younger days that it was mean. It trusted no one. Its ears were generally back on its skull. Its eyes showed white. It gnashed its yellow teeth and it went round in circles in the hope of throwing its hind legs high enough to dash out its chosen victim's brains.

Apart from this, Old Frank, although he pretended otherwise, was inwardly terrified of the beast and, our relative said, no man ever got anywhere with a horse he feared. Fear, he said, advertised itself in voice and touch as well as through the secretions of a man's glands. There was no concealing it. Old Frank was advised not to buy the beast.

We all had supper together that evening, and I got the impression that Frank was going to go against advice and would buy the animal he was sure would make him king of the road, going like a bat out of hell. My aunts, very shrewd young ladies, said Old Frank felt that he was being put off because someone else wanted to step in and buy the fastest horse in the shire. But Old Frank had his secret ambition to fulfil and went off and wasted good money on the rogue pony.

When our relative said he wouldn't have given fivepence for the brute, he really meant it, and he had bought thousands of horses in his time in the local ring to supply the army. What hadn't been done when the pony was broken couldn't be made good now, he said. It remained to be seen, but Frank's new acquisition might well be the death of him.

It was some time before Old Frank came round for supper again. He was huffed, we said, but it wasn't really so. He had gone off and bought a high-wheeled gig and a set of new harness. The pony, we heard on the grapevine, took exception to the harness, snorted and backed and threw up its heels to smash an old churn. It also knocked over a can of skimmed milk and lifted Old Frank off his feet, even though he weighed over 14 stone.

Old Frank still limped when he came over the fields to take supper with us, and out of pity he was driven back to his own farm afterwards. He said nothing about the wild-eyed pony or the new gig. The

115

neighbours had their eye on him. He took the pony and gig round a field one evening and they said it was a miracle he wasn't thrown out and killed. That animal had the devil in him. It snorted fire while Old Frank sat there like a man having a tooth pulled.

Old Frank finally got to the market having loaded the gig with everything about the place except an old blacksmith's anvil that stood in his courtyard. The weight made the wild horse labour and kept the shafts down on his flanks. There were two bags of oats at the fore-end of the gig, some potatoes and a calf in a sack on the floor of the thing. With this cargo the ship came comfortably to port. There was only the journey home.

To fortify himself, Old Frank went to the Black Bull and didn't come out until he was stepping high, red in the face as a turkey. The mean pony was hauled up tight to a ring in the market, but once he was cast off he whirled about and sat Old Frank back in his seat with a thud. The gig left the market on one wheel and covered the first mile of road hardly touching the road between bumps.

People fell back in dismay. A man herding livestock homewards jumped a wall and left his heifers to save themselves. At the bend, where the road goes over the now-derelict railway, the pony was still looking back in anger and frothing at the mouth. It went headlong into the hawthorns like a goshawk in pursuit of its prey, fracturing the shafts of the high-wheeled gig, breaking one of its forelegs and throwing Old Frank out so violently that he was unconscious when people came running to help. Someone got a gun and shot the pony.

Old Frank lost all desire to be the king of the road after that. When he wasn't being conveyed to market at a snail's pace, he would beg a lift from grandfather or one of his friends. There is no point in having a horse if you are afraid of it, he told me solemnly, urging me to bear it in mind. I only need to think of Old Frank, dead these 30 years or more (he lived to a ripe old age taking his own advice), to remember what I already knew. I have always been afraid of spirited horses.

Bunny's Rescue Operation

Bunny must have had some other name, but if he had, I never heard it. In Wales a man may carry a nickname all his life and what he was christened be quite unknown to anyone except his parents, the registrar or schoolteacher. Bunny was Bunny because he made buns. He was one of two village bakers, and made fine bread and better buns.

One thing Bunny loved to do was to get out and fill his lungs with fresh air, and he did this in company with a succession of dogs that he owned over the 20 years or so in which I knew him. The bakehouse life had done nothing for his stomach, he told me on one occasion, and even less for his lungs. Flour gets you in the end, he said; ask any miller.

A day came when I encountered Bunny on the lane with a crowd around him and his dog barking impatiently for the two of them to be on their way and have no more to do with this clamour. It seemed that a small terrier had dived into a kind of minor culvert running under the road. It had been hot on the trail of a rat that had vanished into the cast-iron pipe that debouched water into a ditch. Now the trickle of water had stopped. It seemed that the terrier had been over-keen in plunging after the rat and had got himself stuck up there in the trickling water and the black slime. What was to be done?

Bunny scratched his flour-dusty thatch of hair and considered. Presently he got on his knees in the black ditch and looked up the pipe. There was nothing to be seen but blackness, and the terrier had fallen silent, choked, someone suggested, with black mud. Someone else came hurrying through the small crowd to thrust a long garden cane into Bunny's hand. Bunny poked the cane up the pipe. 'There's something soft up there,' he said. 'It could be his back-end.' Everyone agreed that the dog's back-end was at least five feet towards the middle of the road. Bunny had rolled up his shirt sleeve after taking his jacket off. His naked arm was black right to the shoulder. No one thought he had much chance of poking the poor dog through to the other side, even when someone else suggested getting a clothes prop from a nearby cottage.

Bunny looked at me and wiped mud across his brow with a black hand. He was having another thought, and his audience waited for him to make a pronouncement on the courses open to him. One, he said, was to ring the council. The other was to dig up the road, break through to the wretched dog, and get him out before he died. I knew what it would be. Bunny was a man of action. Talking on a telephone was theory and speculation. Digging up the road with a pick was practical and positive. Bunny called for the pick and shovel to go with it.

When the pick came I noticed that some of those who had been in the forefront had filtered through to the background. They weren't at all sure about digging up the public highway without a by-your-leave or a call to the council to tell them what would be afoot if *they* didn't set a rescue operation in motion right away.

One or two began to mumble about 'the cruelty people', and at least one person said he knew for certain the dog didn't belong to anybody, but Bunny squashed that kind of talk. Cruelty couldn't be allowed to be prolonged while the council met to talk about a hole in the road, and it didn't matter whether the dog had an owner or not. It was a dog, poor wretch. It had to be saved from drowning and suffocation.

Having said this, Bunny proved that he wasn't the pale-faced weakling that a stranger who saw his bakehouse countenance might have thought him to be. He could swing a pick with the best, and to prove it up came great chunks of tarmac and lumps of aggregate. People moved back to 'let the dog see the rabbit', and Bunny, checking the line of the buried pipe, belted away at the hardcore and shovelled it back, making spectators give more ground as the material from the hole was thrown in their direction.

At last Bunny stopped, with a gasp of relief, and announced that he was down at the iron pipe. He called for a heavy hammer so that he could crack the cast iron. Be careful, people said, or you might kill the dog.

It seemed a decided risk, but Bunny, after one or two taps with the heavy hammer, decided that the ring of the pipe at a particular point indicated there was nothing within but the passageway along which the terrier had yet to pass. He began bashing the cast iron for all he was worth, and at length cracked it. There was no sign of the imprisoned dog there or two or three feet on either side of the break-in. Bunny checked again and broke more cast iron without locating the dog. At length our village policeman arrived on the scene, demanding to know 'what was up'. Bunny looked a bit sheepish. The crowd retreated and the policeman took out his notebook to get a few particulars down.

It was while he was doing this that someone saw the mud-covered terrier lying on the grass bank on the other side of the road. It had crawled to safety while everyone was poking and prodding up the pipe or watching Bunny doing his 'road up for repairs' thing. The policeman wasn't impressed but, as he said, it was a matter for the council. It could hardly be said to be wilful damage, could it? Bunny assured everyone that it couldn't.

The trouble was that where the pipe had been smashed, it was impossible to level the road, and the traffic along the lane had to turn back for a whole week before the council did anything about filling in.

The Snare of the Fowler

Old Bob could make any job last. There was no one about the place who could take less out of a ditch with a long-handled shovel than he could without being entirely motionless. No one replaced stones on the dry-stone wall with more deliberation and deep thought. He was the most unhurried man my grandfather ever employed, and he had a sort of phlegmatic way of taking the torrents of abuse that were heaped upon him for his alleged laziness that made less complacent people admire him. He got away with murder, they said. He walked slower than the master and he worked slower than even the boy who knew nothing about the work.

I used to be told to keep away from old Bob because he was slow enough without having me at his elbow as an excuse for going even slower, but Bob was the most interesting man I knew. He was fascinated by the eels he shovelled on to the grass. He would stop and show me the little freshwater shrimps jerking their way into the gravel and he saved 'asps,' which were a particularly thin-bodied green kind of frog, that I might study them for myself. Thanks to Bob, for years I thought an asp was a separate species of frog, and even now I wonder if they weren't part of the magic of my boyhood when the trees were so tall and the razor-backed sows rooted up the little yellow lilies in the field in which old Bob was generally set to clean the ditch.

I am quite sure now that my grandfather was really fond of old Bob and took pity on him, but at that time Bob and I had a sort of conspiratorial friendship. Everything he told me or taught me was in confidence. He could neither read nor write. Everything he had in his head came from pure imagination or from his own experience. He told me that the gedds in the river hated the bitter taste of the toad. It was useless to fish for them with a toad. They weren't fools. They knew a toad when they saw one or they could taste his flavour in the water through which he, and they, swam. I never bothered to try to catch a pike with a toad, but Bob was all for my getting away to the river to catch fish, especially when it was raining heavily.

My grandmother, believe it or not, taught me how to snare a rabbit. Some people would say it was an unladylike thing for a grandmother to do, and it was, considering that she was rather prim and dignified, and

119

even severe, when she combed her hair up, put on her great crow's nest of a hat and rode off with grandfather in the gig to attend the service on Sunday. Old Bob could find nothing wrong with grandmother's teaching. I could snare a rabbit all right. I had even taken a hare with a wire, but had I never heard of the snare of the fowler when the minister was reading from The Book?

Almost at once old Bob brought a single strand of snare wire from the pocket of his buttonless and tattered waistcoat and showed me how to snare a bird. Look see, he said, the pheasant and the little brown bird popped over the bank and through under the fencewire every day. They took shelter in this field and gathered grit in the next, or went there for a dustbath in the morning sun. Even the mallard would weave his way through to the lying corn from the side of the bog, and all the cunning fowler had to do was to study the ground and set his wire in the right place. First time, maybe, the bird would push his way past without getting his head in the noose, but a day would come when he would be brought up sharp in his tracks and hang there for all his struggles and flapping.

I have to admit that an atavistic urge to achieve this end quite put everything else out of my head for a while. I gave up setting snares for rabbits, abandoned all thought of going to the river. I spent a long time studying the comings and goings of pheasants that every morning went promenading on to the old stubble, resplendent in the bright sun, burnished like the copper kettle, crimson-branded, white-marked, and worthy of the fowler's skill, even if a fowler is probably more of a hunter of waterbirds than a catcher of pheasants and ground game. Inevitably I managed the difficult business of snaring a bird. The morning came when the wire wasn't pushed aside or turned back by something that had its head in the noose and cunningly extricated it again. I took the old cock pheasant with my little bit of brass wire depending from the fence, and he waited for me without too much panic until I came within a foot or two of him. He fluffed up and danced a bit then, and a few gold and red feathers floated on the chill October breeze, but it didn't last long. I had him and I marched back to the farm with him with his legs firmly held in both of my hands and at least one gash from his spurs showing red. I was barely seven years old and very proud of myself.

They took the cock pheasant from me. He was looking up sideways at the world the way a bird does when he is held by the feet, and he gaped a little because he was frightened, but he needn't have worried. Almost at once he was launched into the air and set free. He lumbered upwards, got his bearings and went fast out across the little green paddock without a sound save for the heavy beating of his short, almost rounded, wings. It was quite plain, they said, that old Bob was teaching me wicked ways. He would have to be put off the place, sent down the road for corrupting the young. I said nothing. It seemed to me that my grand-mother drew the line between good and evil somewhere between snaring a rabbit and snaring a bird. I may not have retained all my schoolmasters tried to put into my head after that, but I never forgot how to set the snare of the fowler. I could still do it if I needed to, and old Bob has been cleaning the ditches that feed the Styx these many years past.

Encounter with Jack Ty Bach

Jack lived in a small stone house at the tail end of a quarry village, not far from the one in which I lived at the time. It probably had an outside *ty bach,* or privy, of its own, when most of the villagers had to carry water.

Jack Ty Bach was one of those characters whose place in society was hard to define, but certainly was above that of the policeman and near that of the minister and the quarry manager, who were both next to God. I discovered Jack, or he discovered me, when I went to see if there were sea trout at the mouth of the stream. I suspected there might be fish there, and I thought to go down one night after dark and see if one could be taken on a fly.

Jack was there that afternoon, crunching along the shingle in lime-dusty boots, and a little the worse for wear, although I didn't notice this at first. He stopped in his tracks and studied me for a minute. I was taken aback when he seemed to read my mind, for I hadn't a rod or so much as a fishing fly about me. 'They come up,' he said, 'when the tide is in. They can't get past otherwise. Them stones is a barrier they got to get over, so they don't manage it every time. You won't catch them this week, I reckon. The tides is all against it, for you can only get them in the dark.' It is disconcerting to have one's mind read like that. Jack moved off, and it was obvious that he had taken more than an ordinary man's quantity of beer. Not for the first time in my life, I wondered about the truth and a man in drink. Perhaps what we call a befuddled mind is one that focuses on only one thing and with amazing clarity.

After that first encounter I came back and waited for the tide. To tell the truth, the odd sea trout that came over the shingle bar to swim in the shallow water at the mouth of the stream didn't take my fly, and usually went back the way it had come. A worm only produced an eel, but I went on trying. It was like waiting for wigeon in flight, a brief experience with little to show.

Waiting, I occasionally took myself to the pub on the side of the road, through the village. Jack Ty Bach was always there. He could tell I had caught nothing. He patronised me in a kindly way and not because it would get him a free pint. He wanted me to catch a sea trout. It was as though the reputation of the place hung on my succeeding. He told people what I was there for and, sitting himself down beside me, related his life story.

He had gone into the quarry as a boy, working beside his father, whose English was so poor he didn't know the names of the tools and would go about demanding. 'What is shovel?', and stamping in rage when his workmates laughed at him for his inability to learn the old English. 'My father would only keep things he wanted in his head,' he explained. 'His mind was a *cwpwrdd,* you see, with only room for so much. He had no room for a shovel!' Behind the old man's back they called him Jack Shovel, until one day he was killed serving the stone-crusher. Young Jack was left to support his mother and the rest of his family. 'Then the war come and I went off to that,' he said. The war did him no good because he got more than a whiff of gas and came back to work in the quarry hole again. The dust there added to his breathing problems. He drank beer, he said, to 'wash out his tubes'.

On a Saturday when he finished work it sometimes took no fewer than 10 pints to do this. Once, if his cronies were to be believed, it had taken nearly 30. People lost count, and Jack Ty Bach lost all sense of direction, went out to go home and decided to descend a flight of steps to a level nearly 30ft below. The handrail at the top of the flight had been vandalised and Jack stepped off into the air and fell flat onto the road below. He got up, they said, and walked on, but collapsed and was in hospital a month. The ale was a kind of anaesthetic, although the laws of physics, that stuff about the weight and speed of a falling body, applied, and Jack wasn't made of stone.

I asked Jack about his fall and he looked me in the eye, a shy Welsh smile contradicting his usual extrovert character. 'I fell down some steps once. You don't want to believe all they tell you in this place. I never drunk 30 pints. Maybe 15.'

My hopes of ever catching a sea trout at the stream's mouth diminished, and I didn't visit the place for perhaps a month. Jack had been looking for me on a certain Thursday night when the stream was up, the tide was high and sea trout came battering their way over the shingle bar. Boys got them with every kind of device. A woman came down with a galvanised bath and scooped one out of a little tributary of the stream. It was like the magic of midsummer's night and the harvest moon over Snowdon all rolled into one. I hadn't been there, and it might be a year before it happened again, if it ever did.

Jack was disappointed. I called to see him. He wasn't too good. The damp of autumn had begun to get at him, he said. The vapour on the hillside, morning and evening, reminded him of the gas attack in France. He would soon go to lie beside his mother and his poor father who had no room in his head for 'shovel'. I am sure he saw his end as clearly as he saw everything else. He died in November, and for years afterwards they talked about how he drank 30 pints of beer, fell 30ft and got up and walked away as though nothing had happened.

He was, however, something more than a village drunk. He had won a military medal. The minister had a few words to say about it when he buried him. They included the fact that Jack had rescued his officer under fire and displayed outstanding bravery in doing so. With all his talk, Jack never bothered to tell me or anyone else about that. It was sad that people in the village remembered only the 10 pints he drank on a Saturday to 'clear his tubes' and the way he fell from the top of the steps.

The Light in the Window

So that anyone coming up the old road to the farm after dark might have something by which to navigate when there was no moon and the stars were obscured by clouds, it was the custom to keep a light in the window. The farm kitchen, the parlour and the other rooms were all adequately illuminated by oil lamps of one sort or another. The light in the window was a smaller edition of one of these lamps and just big enough to balance on the casement of the kitchen window that 'looked down' the old road.

The glimmer of light was visible at the march gate halfway down the road that eventually reached the public highway just below the cluster of road-end cothouses. There had been occasions when the light served to bring my grandfather safely home even although he lay slumbering on the floor of his gig. His faithful pony steered by it and, when the gates were open, brought his master up into the farm court so that he could be roused and escorted off to bed.

I can remember many occasions when, coming back to the farm at New Year or for some special family get-together, the light in the window was a sight that brought a sudden lump to my throat. I immediately imagined the snugness of the farm kitchen, the scent of burning peat and the glitter of burnished brass.

More than once in my teens I came up the road in the small hours and blessed the fact that the light was burning in the window. It wasn't lit unless someone was away or someone was expected, but it was a significant beacon. It meant that the door was unlocked. There was really no need to lock the door of course, for anyone entering the kitchen would never get out. The dogs would see to that.

Travelling abroad by night in those days generally meant going in the gig, which had candle-lit, brass giglamps, or riding a bicycle equipped with a carbide lamp. Often the gale blew the giglamps out and the carbide let the rider down. A traveller on foot had nothing to worry about except perhaps getting past the tree where a tinker had supposedly hanged himself, or a place where a suicide had jumped into the river.

The window light was comforting, for when it came into view the journey in darkness was almost at an end.

I can remember a character who was employed as a ploughman having the lamp lit for him once, then twice a week, and finally the lamp being blown out on him because he had gone beyond the bounds of common decency. He was one of a number of 'Wee Johnnies' employed over the years. I can't remember ever hearing of a Wee Willie, except the one who went to bed by candlelight, but because my grandfather was known to some people as Big John, anyone he employed with the same Christian name as his own became Wee Johnnie.

This particular Wee Johnnie was fond of the bright lights. He loved the atmosphere of a place called the Half-way House at the tail end of the village, and when he could induce my aunts to make him a loan against his term day settlement of wages, he would be off to the inn as fast as his short legs would carry him. Here, in the bar, he would fall in with others of a similar disposition who had walked in from remote farms, feeling the need for human contact and cultivating a thirst in the process.

Wee Johnnie's love of schooners and chasers was frowned upon. He would come to a bad end, he was told, when he hurried in from his stint on the milking stool after feeding and grooming his team, but he paid little attention. He was away in his mind, enjoying the 'crack' and the

124

jokes, and feeling a warm glow spreading through his system. He worked hard enough, and he was on the long walk of the ploughmen, a walk that began after harvest and went right on through the winter, and well into spring, for then there was harrowing and drilling to be done. If he could face a five-mile walk for a dram, why shouldn't he have his drink?

The lamp began to serve Wee Johnnie as a kind of lighthouse, however. He became steadily more the worse for wear when he came back, and he began to go more frequently, falling in with cattle dealers who always seemed to have more money to spend. The light burned more frequently for Wee Johnnie than it did for members of the family who went visiting, and certainly more often for him than for his master, whose excursions were infrequent. Wee Johnnie would present himself for his breakfast looking sadly the worse for his night out, and sometimes with cuts and bruises acquired in collision with hawthorn trees along the Devil's Elbow.

He was warned with all seriousness that one night he would miss his way and step into the black water of the river below the distillery, as a farmer friend of my grandfather's had done, but Wee Johnnie had heard it all before. There was no joy in a life without the prospect of walking into the Half-way House and being greeted with the kind of affection and warmth he had come to know.

Alas, the habit began to overtax even his iron constitution. It seemed that if he continued to walk in the dark and navigate by the lamp in the window he would never finish the long walk behind the plough. He was

125

warned that it was no way to go on and that he sat in to milk in the morning, not to doze against the warm flank of an Ayrshire cow. The light in the window wouldn't be lit for him anymore. It had once caught fire as the wick sooted up. The house could have been burned down.

Wee Johnnie stayed out a night or two, and that was the very end. I sometimes wondered what he felt about it all when he became one of the town drunks. He never managed to see the light again. I was always sorry for him, for he was a candidate to be a pedestrian Tam o' Shanter.

The Vanished Rope-rollers

One of the arts of which the farm worker was once very proud was rick-building. By the time harvest was in, the rickyard would be almost completely filled and every set of staddles occupied by neatly-built corn ricks. A good hay rick was much harder to build by the nature of things, since hay was forked loose from wagon or cart, and the building took considerable knowledge of how to lay the perimeter layer and keep the heart of the rick evenly filled, without the whole thing becoming lop-sided, out of symmetry, or developing a shape that the wind would soon change.

A hay rick would be raked, and occasionally banged and bolstered into shape as its height increased. The perfect shape tapered outwards gently from the staddles or the boulder base to a rotundity that was as pleasing a shape as that of a large barrel of beer. At its maximum diameter, which depended upon the diameter of the base, it tapered more abruptly inwards again as it rose to the cone of its top, all of which would be thatched with freshly brought-in sheaves of round rushes. A corn rick's construction began with the placing of sheaves, butts outwards on the perimeter of the foundation. Occasionally there would be a sort of flooring of straw to preserve the evenness of the rise of the rick, as layer after layer of sheaves went on, with inner sheaves head to tail. The heart of a corn rick was sometimes deeper. One could slip down to the thigh in it if its construction wasn't properly managed. The shape of the rotund rick was more easily preserved by the fact that sheaves had even butts. A corn rick could be built higher. It didn't sink or slump the way a badly built hayrick would in a matter of months. It, too, was thatched with round rushes. Finally, the fringe of the thatch was neatly trimmed.

Rick thatches were held on by the network of ropes that encompassed the cone. Four ladders were used. They were special rick ladders kept at other times in the longest barn or outhouse, and were brought out only twice in a season, when the thatching was done and when the threshing was due. It was one thing to thatch, but no great problem to scale the bleached covering of rushes away from the corn rick when that needed to be done. Both operations, however, required some patient work making or taking apart the rope network covering the cone, like a sort of open-weave lady's hairnet. Tidiness in the rickyard might be a matter of final touches (raking, cutting, putting a top-knot on each of the well-matched ricks that lined the path), but the business of roping the rick required order.

At the end of a season, or after a big threshing, there would be a tangle of ropes to be gathered up and untangled. The ropes were known as grassropes. They were not particularly strong, and were made of a fibrous material like coconut hair and not sisal, from which some cart ropes, although not the plough lines, were woven. The tangled grass-ropes would be bundled off to a high granary and left on the floor, where they would dry out. On wet days, those with nothing to do were sent to 'roll' ropes.

Since some of the ropes had been passed round and round the thatched cone of a corn rick, and knotted here and there, while others had stretched vertically from the very top to a foot or so from the ground (the whole network and thatch was held firm by dangling ventilated bricks, drain tiles or shiny, well-polished curling stones) there were many knots to be undone. When a beginning and an end were discovered, the length of rope would be coiled, the person making the coil looping it through between thumb and fingers and behind his elbow in quick and expert loops that supported the rolling. The final result was a tapered, not too fat and certainly symmetrical coil of rope. Unless this rolling was neatly executed the 'netting' of the rick next season would be made clumsy and difficult, a fat coil having to be pushed under and over the verticals weighted with tiles or stones.

Before hay harvest the high granary would be tidy and the grassropes stacked ready to be brought out and used again. Even a straw stack, which was generally a problem because of the unmanageability of straw that came tumbling out of the threshing machine and had to be hurriedly raked and forked back out of the way, could be squared and made almost as pleasing to the eye as a rectangular building.

Straw was generally built into what we called sow stacks, not because they slumped like an old sow wallowing in a midden, but because they tended to be long. No one built three or four straw stacks, when as many

127

corn stacks were being threshed out. The straw went into one long 'building' for which there would be a rearrangement of the stackyard boulders to accommodate the rectangle—if a permanent base for a straw stack couldn't be kept in readiness. The straw stack, too, would be roped. All the stack ladders would be brought out for this, and there would be a roper on each ready to receive the coil of grassrope as it was passed to him, loop it under and over the vertical and pass it to the next man.

Now in the countryside the rickyard is a thing of the past. Straw is pounded into bales and banded with twine like the hair of a pig. The corn is already threshed and goes to the drier because it never stands to dry on the stook. There was a beauty about the rickyard I have never ceased to treasure in my mind.

Tall Tales of Strong Men

While I never thought about it when I was a child, it strikes me now that the legend of the strong man was necessary in the hard world of yesterday. The old people talked of him and embellished their stories with new details as they handed them on to another generation.

It was a rather odd thing that no one had ever met the folk hero, but their grandfather had known him, they seemed to recall, and there had been no one like him since. He had carried enormous sacks of flour up the mill stairs, despising the chain and winch. His heart, had he been anything but the superman he was, must have burst with the burden he put upon it. Sometimes he even ran up the steps, and worked all day from morning until night without stopping. He appeared when a wagon was tipped over into the ditch, put his great shoulder to the wheel, and, with the veins on his neck standing like blue ropes, he heaved the whole thing back on to the road.

Great-grandfather had witnessed the feat. It had happened on the road to so-and-so. It had also happened on the road to several other places, but of course the people who told this version had the location wrong. Sometimes they also got the name wrong. In our version it was a giant of a man called Old Ertle, and Old Ertle had travelled far and wide, performing all kinds of feats of strength. There had been a time when, on a long journey from one side of the shire to the other, his poor little pony had been unable to carry him. He was a big man, it seemed, and when the pony couldn't even carry itself up the hills he ducked his head under its belly, grabbed it by a foreleg and a hindleg and carried it the rest of the way.

My great-grandfather had encountered Old Ertle, marching through the village with the pony across his shoulders, and the superman had stopped for 'a crack' without putting the animal down. They were that kind of man in those days I was told. I could believe it because none of my elders doubted it for a moment, and we children sat around listening with eyes bulging as the legend unfolded.

There were a lot of very powerful men working on the land at a time when horsepower was counted from one to three, with maybe five as the limit. It was the kind of life that sorted the weak from the strong, and not just the men from the boys. Those who hadn't inherited strength went to the wall and were discounted. Strong men were hired at the fair. Farmers felt their muscles and prodded them as they prodded the beast in the ring.

There was a Doric word for a strong man. He was a *yall* one. This meant that he was as indestructible as an oak post, as powerful as a horse. It implied that he was strong in the head as well as in the arm, I think. The word was reserved for a man everyone admired. He was a fellow who could fork all day at a threshing, mow from morning until night, carry corn to the granary until further orders, and swing churns on to a cart unaided, no matter how heavy they were. A horse was never *yall*. A mere boy could never be so. There were no *yall* women, and *yall* men became legends.

It seemed we had had a few in our own family, although I began to wonder about the whole thing when I was 10 or 12 years old. A great-uncle, who considered himself one of the best story-tellers in the shire, told me how grandfather had made his own legend by carrying an enormous boulder from one side of a particular road to dump it on the other, with the immodest remark, 'And let a better man carry it back!' My great-uncle was unable to explain exactly why grandfather had found it necessary to lift that great boulder and stagger with it from one side of the road to the other. He looked rather disgusted with me when I said I knew the place. I had seen the stone and could never work out why anyone as sensible and practical as his brother ever thought of moving the boulder when it would have done just as well on one side of the road as the other. I had killed a new legend in the making. I had refused to look at it with the imagination of my forebears. I had asked a fool question.

There was a touch of mischief in me even at that age, I suppose, because I had another version of the legend concerning that stone. Old Ertle himself had lifted it from one side of the road to the other, according to grandfather, and for no apparent reason. But Old Ertle, I had been told, like all supermen, never did anything just for the sake of showing off. He carried his pony because the pony was tired. All the other wonderful things he had done had been things in urgent need of doing. Was it on one of his off days that he had picked up the boulder and carried it across the road? I began to think he had never done it.

When my great-uncle brought the legend into his own generation, attributing this and other feats to our own family, he made me wonder about many old tales. I didn't believe in Santa Claus, but I was more sadly disillusioned over the supermen, the mighty blacksmiths, the millers, and men standing in the shadow of giants like Old Ertle.

I have lived a little longer now, and I confess I find myself creating my own legend. There was a time when our herd of Ayrshires were infected with some sort of bug that made their eyes and noses run. The vet came and prescribed treatment which had to be administered to them all once every day. The milkers were hauled up tight in their stalls and had their eyes washed and their nostrils syringed, but the bull who accompanied them was free. He was never chained, but stood in an open stall, waiting for his harem to be milked and then accompanying them back to the pasture. Each day grandfather would walk up to that massive beast, catch him by the head, throw much more than a ton of bull off its legs and hold it on the ground while the stockman or byreboy gave the treatment.

Was it what is called knack or was the old ex-blacksmith the last of the supermen? All I can say is that the bull was full-grown and resisted, although he never came off best. Even Old Ertle couldn't have made a better job of it, and maybe, after all, he did have some reason for lifting that boulder from one side of the road to the other and did carry his pony on his back.

A Poacher's Passing

To have news of happenings in my old village is one of my greatest pleasures. When one has lived in a place for more than twenty years the news of its daily life continues to have a strong appeal, but last week it was sad news. Hughie Bach, poacher and casual labourer, was dead.

This week the local farmers gave him 'a wonderful funeral, fair play to them,' and everyone smiled sadly at their recollections of Hughie Bach, whose like we shall never see again. I learned of his death when I overheard someone saying that another little man walking up the village street reminded him of Hughie Bach. The past tense made me prick up my ears.

Hughie Bach was somewhere around sixty-seven to sixty-nine. They say he had no National Insurance card, and probably he didn't carry his birth certificate with him. He couldn't last for ever, but he hadn't changed in all the years I had known him. So they might be wrong. He might have been much older. He was no more than five feet high, and he had round, innocent eyes. A child-like innocence was always upon his face. All his clothes were too big for him, for they were hand-me-downs given to him by whatever farmer was employing him when his trousers, jacket, boots or coat gave out. His standard apparel in winter was an over-sized Home Guard greatcoat that was tied at the waist with binder twine. He generally wore the collar of the greatcoat turned up and his earth-stained cap, tugged slightly askew over his left eye, gave him the appearance of a peasant general of a rabble army, until one saw the dog at his heels.

Hughie's dog was always as nondescript as he was, but it changed now and again, for he would sell his dog into the hands of the Philistines without hesitation. The dog kept him company in whatever barn happened to be his sleeping quarters and went down to the village with him to his favourite ale house, attached to his wrist by a length of binder-twine. When things got difficult and no one would give Hughie any more than his daily bread, and his thirst became intolerable, he launched a campaign to sell his current dog, knowing well that anyone intoxicated enough to buy the dog would soon part with it when he sobered up, on account of the dog's natural habits and self-evident parasites. If and when this happened, Hughie and his dog would be reunited.

There was something child-like about Hughie. When he had got drunk and he found he still had a sixpence, the first child he met, as he swayed and staggered out of the village, received his bounty. He had that harmless Welsh weakness of imagining that because he was of the blood he could sing, but what a painful sound was Hughie's singing! The birds deserted the eaves when he sang and dogs threw up their heads and howled. To watch Hughie's comings and going was to be entertained. His boots stayed on his feet only by the grace of Providence and he scuffed along at a great pace when he went to quench his thirst. But

131

when he came back the urgency had gone out of his life and his concern then was to proceed by easy stages and to stay more or less vertical. The iron railings along the side of the glen opposite my house were a blessing to him, particularly when he lurched off the kerb, spun on his heel and began to tumble. Always, as though by a miracle, he reached out and made one frightening, perilous stride that enabled his fat little hand to grab support and prevent a fall. There he would hang until the conifers beyond the railings ceased to drift away and then he would let go and take another short pace as before. Every short pace ended in a sudden gyration, a lurch, a spin and a frantic clutch at the railings. It was my constant concern that he might fall flat on his face, and the boys who followed at a distance always hoped that he would provide them with this final laugh.

Being his own master, Hughie seemed to govern his life by market-day excursions. He knew he could get lifts and in the neighbouring market towns he was bound to earn a shilling helping someone to load or unload livestock. The hardships of his uncomfortable world were dispelled by the generosity of farmers and country folk who knew him well, and once he had the price of a drink he was set for the rest of the day.

My first meeting with Hughie took place long ago when I went up, at the request of a farmer, to shoot some pigeons feeding on his newly seeded wheat. Stalking carefully along the side of the field, I became aware that someone else was doing the same thing and coming in my direction. I stood behind a thorn until he almost walked into me and Hughie Bach's innocent eyes almost popped out of his head. In a little while we were talking freely to each other and he asked to see my gun, a rather handsome hammerless ejector.

By way of exchange he allowed me to examine his piece. It had come from the corner of a stable or from down the back of a corn chest. It rattled and it was nearly impossible to see the sky through its barrel. I don't think Hughie used it that day, or we shouldn't have had his funeral this week. We talked about game and the life of the fields and a fox in a glass case that the farmer was using as a scarecrow. Our intimacy was extraordinary, but it was never renewed.

From that day on Hughie touched his cap to me and smiled his broken-toothed smile. I became one of those on his list. He toasted my health if ever we met in one of his quiet, out-of-the-way drinking haunts. Sometimes he came to me and made conspiratorial approach on the subject of partridges and pheasants he hoped to bag, or could put me in the way of for a shilling. But by Hughie's standards I was an amateur.

132

He lived so close to the earth that his body warmed it and he had all the natural cunning of a man living in that fashion.

There was a time when they talked of potato rationing and one night shortly after it was mooted I chanced upon Hughie at a quiet country inn where I had gone in the company of three friends. Hughie was singing one of his high-pitched, off-key dirges, but soon he drifted over to my elbow to ask if I wanted a sack of potatoes 'just in case.' There was drama in the air. Hughie left straight away and I followed a minute or two later with my friends in tow.

As soon as I said I would buy the potatoes, which he assured me were part of his perks for assisting at the lifting of the crop, Hughie urged us to get into the car and he would guide us to the place where the potatoes waited. We travelled through a network of lanes. It was a very dark night and a little drizzle was falling, but at length we reached the place and Hughie got out of the car and disappeared into the darkness. We put the headlights out and waited. He was so long away that we were on the point of giving him up when at last he staggered down the bank with the sack of potatoes, which he dumped into the boot of the car. I thought it odd that he wasn't disposed to accept a lift back. As soon as he had the money in his hands he sped away, but when we opened the sack at home we knew the reason. We had perhaps twenty pounds of potatoes, and eighty pounds of rock which we didn't bother to divide!

The next time I saw Hughie I expected to detect just a flicker of conscience in his expression, but there was none. He was bland, he was innocent, and he taught me that a true son of nature doesn't live in the past and experience is carried only if it doesn't undermine self-confidence.

There are many stories I could tell of Hughie's misdeeds and brushes with authority but *de mortuis* . . . The farmers for whom he had worked, and who had so often tolerated his wayward habits and shortcomings, nevertheless thought a lot of him. They saw his remains decently interred and stood by his grave, each one aware, as the whole village is aware, that here was a unique character. It is certain that this generation or the next won't throw up another Hughie Bach.

Latter-Day Nero

Although I wasn't there when little Johnnie Kee, the fiddler, set fire to the barn, because I had been taken south to live with my mother and father, I remember the letter that came telling of the near disaster. I knew the culprit well. He was one of those itinerant 'workers' who would arrive for casual employment at turnip-thinning, threshing, haymaking, harvest or potato-gathering.

Little Kee was not a very robust character, and he was generally to be found dodging in the lee of the threshing machine or behind the drystone wall while others were working hard. He wouldn't have been taken on except that he had a wheedling, persuasive way with him, and my grandparents always had a soft spot for people who belonged nowhere and lived the hard life. In the six or seven years he came knocking at the door, I doubt whether he had done as much as a full week's work, but he had had countless breakfasts, dinners and suppers, and slept months in the barn or the strawhouse.

My aunts always laughed to see his diminutive figure hurrying to keep pace with their father as he plodded up the steading. They always knew what it was about when the 'wee sparrow' was pestering the 'crow'. The little man ingratiated himself with grandfather. He would come hurrying to the kitchen door to say that 'the master' had told him he was to have a cup of tea and a scone and jam as a mid-morning snack. If the lassies liked, he would get his fiddle and play them a tune.

Outraged though they might well have been, my aunts would comply with 'the master's' instruction. Little Kee would go ricketing across the steading for his fiddle, and play them a tune while the tea was made. He was forbidden to take the fiddle to the field, however, for grandfather had once found his haymakers cavorting to the strains of a reel instead of working, and had laid down the law about it.

Few of the other itinerants who came enjoyed such privileges. Although grandfather was a notoriously hard taskmaster when his harvest was threatened by bad weather, he had a soft spot that let Johnnie Kee get away with it. The little man was sometimes invited in in the evening to play, and would go through his repertoire of well-loved tunes and sing ballads that should really have been set down on paper as folk music.

I remember being there when great-aunt Ellen came on a visit at a time when Wee Johnnie Kee was sleeping in the barn. Great-aunt Ellen was a grand lady and had to have the best bedroom, which was downstairs. She would complain that she couldn't get to sleep for the sound of owls or a dog barking miles away, and on this memorable night she became alarmed when the silence was broken by the sound of a violin.

No one had mentioned that there was someone sleeping in the barn, much less that someone would play a tune in the small hours! My aunts, who knew all about it, weren't troubled. They said Wee Johnnie played to an audience of rats, and I had a childish vision of whiskered, bright-eyed rats sitting on their haunches, charmed by the music.

Great-aunt Ellen roused the household convinced that the place was haunted. Could it be otherwise with the sound of a violin and the dog whining at the door? She never met Wee Johnnie. She would have dabbed her aquiline nose with a lavender-scented handkerchief had she done so, and wouldn't have stayed downwind of him for long.

My mother wasn't too happy about the occasional tenant of the barn when she came to stay, and my aunts generally managed to get Wee Johnnie moved out when mother was due. It was all very well serving him ham and eggs, and there was always enough to spare both at dinner and supper time, but no visitor could rest content in their bed with someone drifting about the outbuildings like a grey ghost in woollen drawers.

Ballad-singers and fiddlers were really well out of their time, and grandfather was being perverse in encouraging the scraggy, shiftless little man to stay, even if his visits were seasonal. He really wasn't much use, for he was too small for a hayfork or a rake, and barely the size of a good sheaf of corn. He had a struggle to carry a can of potatoes. Wee Johnnie continued to come, however, and then, although I never saw the going of him, he went.

The letter that told us of his final escapade said that his insomnia, brought on by the fact that he never did enough work to get tired and need sleep, had got worse. He would walk about and play his fiddle and smoke his clay pipe through the night until cockcrow, and then, when he saw the first trickle of smoke from the chimney, would knock on the door for a cup of tea. A spark from the clay pipe must have fallen into the chaff before Wee Johnnie climbed into his tattered trousers. Alarmed at what he saw, the little man took to his heels. By all accounts he didn't stop until he was miles away and his socks and woollen underwear soaked with the heavy dew that had fallen. Like Nero, he had kept his hold on his fiddle even if he left his trousers and boots behind. He never came back.

Fortunately, the smoke from the barn was spotted and a chain of water buckets organised to enable the flames to be put out. It was no joke. The barn roof was holed and had to be re-timbered and re-slated. The policeman was sent on the trail of Wee Johnnie, but the fiddler had managed to find clothes to fit him and made his escape. He had the distinction of being the very last itinerant allowed to sleep in the barn.

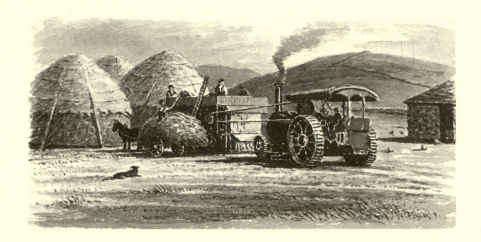

The Fall of Wee Bachal

Bachal—or Bauchal—means a small boy or little one (in Welsh, a *Bachgen*), although in my childhood I was accustomed to hearing the word applied to a person of below average height and almost invariably someone who walked on the outer edges of their feet. Yon wee bachal were words of pity mingled with disapproval, but for me the Wee Bachal who epitomised all bachals was a character who for a long time was one of the loungers at the corner of the town square.

The Bachal had come down in the world in my lifetime of six or seven years, for I had encountered him in a high position before I found him again at the corner among the loungers. When he was almost a god he occupied the platform or firestep of the great engine that hauled the threshing machine from farm to farm each autumn and on into winter when weather permitted. He had been engine driver to the threshing

136

contractor for the whole of his working life and was known as the Bachal because he was barely 5 feet tall.

When he was up there, turning the big wheel that steered the mammoth engine about the road and through the court to the rickyard, the Bachal's lack of inches went unnoticed. His short legs were overlooked. His broad and rotund figure should have been fitted with legs of appropriate length, for his body was that of a large man. Indeed, the black serge suit he wore had been made for such a man. His trousers were cut off at ground level to hide his small feet, which, nevertheless, bulged and overhung his shapeless footwear.

I could not understand how a man who had had so much power and glory had come to be content leaning against a wall at the corner of the square beside people like Big Willie and Butcher Murphy, who, after all, were professional idlers of lifelong experience.

The Bachal had worked hard. His serge suit bore testimony to his industry, long after he had given up, for it was glazed with a coating of engine grease and soot that looked like blacklead. His engineer's cap with a vizor had worn away the hair at his temples, and yet, when he was among the idlers, it belied his total idleness and made him look like a man who was resting for a short while.

There was something else about the sawn-off proportions of the Bachal that made him look better than work-shy. It was the way he kept his jacket swept back and his thumbs in the armholes of his waistcoat. I always felt that he stood there cooling off, waiting for the threshing-day gang of workers to finish their soup or their bowls of tea and jam scones before he hauled himself back up and pushed the lever to set the threshing machine in motion once again. Then the whole monster flailed and rumbled and turned out a great endless sausage of straw, sacks of corn and mountains of chaff.

'Who was on the corner today?' someone would ask when we came in after putting the gig in the gighouse and stabling the pony. We gave a brief list of the loungers and other town characters we had seen. 'Yon wee Bachal was there,' we would add, and talk about his day as master of that great train when he blew the whistle, mopped the fat belly of the thing with an oily rag he often used to mop his own fat, boyish face with, and played at being lord of all he surveyed.

The Bachal had loved his work and had seen thousands of harvests through the mill, drunk thousands of gallons of tea to wash down dust and chaff, and slept in his cabin in hundreds of different places from one end of the shire to the other. Why then had the mighty fallen and how had he come to join the weathermen on the corner of the square, retreating into the shelter of eaves and porch when it rained, and coming out again as the sun began to shine and dogs lay once again on sandstone doorsteps?

His wife, it seemed, had left him for a tinker who had come round the doors while the Bachal was away on tour one autumn. The Bachal had come home, weeks later, all the corn threshed and money in his pocket, to find his house deserted and a kettle deep in ash in the middle of a rusting range. He had gone up the street to the public house and stayed there, sleeping in the mews between whiles and drowning his sorrows. It was a miserable winter and a long time before his employers had much need for the mobile unit the Bachal usually navigated about the roads.

When they called him in he was in no state to take his 'ship' to sea, his great fuming monster over the hills and through the hollows of the remote countryside. He was pickled in spirit and far gone in alcoholism. They looked at his unhealthy pallor, the sweat on his yellowing brow and told him they couldn't risk the equipment under his command any longer. The Bachal went back to the square, rubbed elbows with the professionals and never worked again.

Once in a while when a farmer came in to transact some piece of business the Bachal stood up straight, tugged at his greasy cap and bade the gentleman good-day, asking what kind of harvest he expected, or how many ricks he had threshed. He died before the more celebrated of the permanently unemployed. I remember hearing someone say that his coffin was short and broad because he had been a big man with short legs, a right bachal of a body.

The Man Who Came to Mow

There were several scythes that were kept hanging in the barn against the day when it was impossible to find anything better for the 'boy' to do but send him out to cut thistles, but when Wee Johnnie came to us at the very beginning of harvest he brought his own. He carried it on his back with a bit of sacking wrapped round the blade in case he stumbled and cut himself. He looked like a soldier from the past, and the way he could use the scythe would have made him a formidable adversary even for a man with a claymore. Wee Johnnie wasn't tall, but crablike, his legs seeming to be not much longer than his arms. He was the best mower for thirty miles, a day's travel in the horse age.

The corn would just be turning colour when he arrived. The stubble was always bleaching by the time he departed. When he left, the rickyard was a lovely sight—two straight lines of portly ricks, each with a fine network of grassrope to hold the thatch down, and the tail ends of the ropework weighted with drain tiles, ventilated bricks or old curling stones. Wee Johnnie 'opened the roads'—cut the pathway round the perimeter of the field and sometimes across it in two or three places—so that the corn binder could get in and do its work.

It wasn't that the harvesters we gathered about us couldn't put their hand to the scythe and make a fair job of opening roads. The average farm labourer could mow if he had to, but the mowing tended to be like the barber's work, a bit patchy and not tidy. Wee Johnnie could accomplish more in the morning before the tea basket arrived than most other men could mow in a whole day. So he came to mow, open roads, mow round rocks and rough knolls, cut lying corn and keep everything so tidied up that the machine or machines could clatter round at top speed and make the most of the task they were specifically designed for. Johnnie's mowing of soft ground averted the danger of the machine bogging down, he saved a lot of time and prayers to the Almighty to prevent such disasters. When the corn was cut and stooked Wee Johnnie was away in the bog fields, cutting round rushes for thatch.

He never did anything but mow. Mowing was, as far as I knew, his trade, although what he did between harvests I can't imagine. He was known as a mower. Perhaps in his own corner of the outback he was known as a poacher, a builder of walls, a catcher of moles. His skill was with the scythe. Nothing else he did matched his reputation as a mower.

I can remember tagging along behind Wee Johnnie, fascinated by the evenness of the stubble he left behind him, the neatness of corn, thistles and yellow weeds all laid in a swath to one side. It was something beautiful to watch, and the rhythm of his stride, the way he moved, was like a dance, a graceful movement that changed almost imperceptibly as he went on. He stopped only once in a while to take the sharpening stone from his hip pocket, wave it across the black and shining iron of the blade, and put the thing back in his pocket again with the same grace.

He was one of the last of a special breed, a man who had cut whole fields of corn in his day, whole fields of hay, countless acres of round rushes. His scythe was personal, set to suit his body and his stride, no doubt. The uncanny thing was that although he achieved so much, he didn't seem to hurry. In the morning he would stop for the tea basket. In the afternoon he would have two or three stops on his own account, to mop his brow and drink water mixed with fine oatmeal, using a bowl

139

which was left beside the white enamelled pail brought to the field exclusively for Wee Johnnie's use.

When I dogged his heels he would sometimes tell me to look for the nest of a fieldmouse he had just passed over, or the olive eggshells in what had been a pheasant's nest. He spared the sleeping or petrified hare and only turned his head to smile when a brood of young partridges exploded to left or right of his route.

I wanted to be a mower myself for a while. It seemed to be the easiest thing to do. Out there in the field the sun was always shining, birds perched on swaying stalks, pigeons went slowly across the sea of corn and grasshoppers sang on the sunny hillocks that rose from oats or barley. I loved to go down to the bog field and take Wee Johnnie his tea. Down there he never suffered the same thirst as he did in the harvest field and didn't have his oatmeal and water. The going was uneven and there were many other things to be seen—paddocks (toads) that worked their way through the forest of stalks, waterhens that left tracks on the black earth, snipe that rose and cut their way like sickles slashing at the sky, and the odd wild duck that circled before departing.

I would have been a mower, just as I would have been a plasterer when I watched one mend the ceiling of the cheese loft with a few smooth strokes after the quick turn of a trowel. I didn't understand that men are born with special abilities. A sower had a leg-length and an arm-length particularly suited to sowing corn. These attributes, the size of the hand to pick up the grain, the regular stride, made a sower. The dimensions of a man and the articulation of his limbs made a mower —these things, and years and years of practice. There simply cannot be mowers like Wee Johnnie anywhere in Britain today. We have no time for them, no use for them. I like to think that he walked right on, cutting his road, leaving an even stubble, a neat swath, all the way to the end of it, and then disappeared like the morning star disappears, with the daylight.

The Artful Dodger

My snapshot of Wee Pat working in the harvest field, preserved in a collection of similar, faded photographs, does not do him justice, but it shows that he wasn't always talking and sometimes went through the motions of a day's work. He came to us with three other harvesters from 'across the water', contracted men engaged every year to help get the corn home.

I can remember when Pat showed up. The other three men arrived according to the arrangement with the man who found them work in Galloway, but Pat, although he had travelled on the same boat, contrived to get left behind. He caught a later train. He walked all the way from the station and it took him three hours. Fortunately for him there was no work that day. 'Sor,' he said, 'it's late I am today but tomorrow I'll be early, and if you like to look at it that way, I'm early for tomorrow today.' Everyone laughed. We were expected to laugh. Wee Pat was artful. He knew his way of saying things, the way he cocked his head and looked up to see the effect, charmed everyone.

He was always respectful and always admitted his shortcomings and his guilt. He was a half-pint of a man, another Wee Bauchal, who had never grown up physically. He bustled about. He was animated. It was difficult to discover what he achieved, but his 'crack' was wonderful. He had a thousand stories, and to hear him he had lived through the famine, eating grass. He had come into this world with nothing, he said, and would go out of it with nothing. To prove it, he would pull out the linings of all his pockets. He kept his little clay pipe and his twist of tobacco in his waistcoat, and, I think, a few other things in those same pockets that were never turned out to demonstrate that his life was one of penury.

I suppose if they had stood side by side, my grandfather would have towered more than a foot above the little man's head. When he ordered Wee Pat to do something he expected him to jump, but when Pat got it wrong he was amazingly tolerant with him. The one thing he couldn't bear was being called 'sor'. 'And Pat,' he would say, 'we'll have no more of the sors!' Wee Pat would touch his cap and say, 'Very well, sor. You are the master, sor!' and in the very next breath it would be 'sor' once again.

No one ever thought that we were stuck with Wee Pat. He had no intention of ever going back to that green land across the sea. The harvest drew to an end. There were only the ricks to be thatched. The three very industrious Irishmen who had reached us ahead of Pat respectfully took their leave and caught the first available boat, but Pat didn't roll his bundle when they rolled theirs. 'Sor,' he said, 'I am not a man to leave anybody in the lurch. I will stay. I will help your men thatch them stacks. I will lift your pratees for you, and see it through, and I'll ask for nothing but me bowl of soup and me dinner.' He had to be hired. He had nobody in this world. All his relatives had died. His

141

only son had gone off to America and never written a word. Where would he find the comfort of a fire and kindness?

And so he stayed and was as happy as a sandboy. He overfed the pigs and the hens. He slipped on the midden plank and had to have all his clothes boiled in the setpot while he sat by the fire, wrapped in a blanket and wearing an outsized set of woollen combinations.

Grandfather cured him of his 'sors' in time. He never liked the word because, he said, it was Erse for pig, and you never knew with a bag of monkeys like Wee Pat! Nevertheless there was a decided paternal feeling towards the little man, who was, I think, almost the same age as his new-found employer. Wee Pat became a kind of family mascot in whom we discovered hidden talent. If he couldn't yoke a big Clydesdale in a cart without almost braining himself with the shaft, or getting his own foot pinned to the ground by the animal's enormous hoof, he could play the melodeon. No one ever discovered where the instrument came from. He hadn't had it when he arrived, but all at once there was music from the stable where Pat sat on the corn chest playing Irish tunes.

I suppose Pat would have remained with the family until time was with him no more, but he was sent to cart coals from the station. In those days coal had begun to take the place of peat from our rented moss. Now what peat was brought down was reserved for the parlour fire. Coal fuelled the range, although the embers were always covered with wood when cooking had to be done. The economic way was to buy a truckload of coal and cart it home. The 30 tons, or whatever it was, involved several days of carting because the nearest station was quite a long way off. It seemed a job for Wee Pat and off he went to bring the first load.

The load he brought was a small one. He had complied with grandfather's instruction to drop off a few generous shovelfuls at poor old so-and-so's door, and some to keep another cottager warm. The next load was no greater, however. Pat said something about coal sliding from the truck and having to be shovelled up from the ground, and he wasn't a very 'high' man. The next day he brought only one small load and was inexplicably the worse for wear. On the third day he didn't get back until after milking time and he brought no coal at all. He had spent most of the day in the pub having sold as much coal as would keep him in drink: 'But sor, tomorrow sor, I'll make up for it . . .' Alas, he had distributed more coal than remained to be brought home.

Charity begins at home, and so he went, off down the road, his bundle on his back with the melodeon tied to it. We never saw or heard of him again.

With Sawdust in His Moustache

We always went 'down' to the Hillhead because it was situated down at the end of the farm road. It was Hillhead because it stood on a little brow, above the 'public' road. Hillhead comprised five cottages and the joiner's 'shop', which was a sizeable, high tarred shed in which the joiner had his workbench and a belt-driven saw.

There, up to his knees in pine shavings, the joiner made a settle, gathered beech sawdust on his eyebrows and moustache as he shaped a spoke or a shaft, and lived, in my eyes at least, the life of a king, a man who could make anything from a coffin to a cart, a stair to the loft, or a meal chest for the kitchen. He was what we called a Fifer, came from that Kingdom to the Kingdom of Galloway and speaking with a broad accent more readily detectable than the accent of the men of Kyle across our northern frontier. It was that kind of world, of course. People mostly only travelled for wars or to escape their debtors and moral responsibilities.

The joiner always made fun of me in a kindly fashion. He would pick me up and place me carefully out of his way so that he could operate one or other of his many pieces of machinery or I would get my toes cut off by the morticing machine, my head taken off by the slapping belt that criss-crossed on its way in and out of the workshop. The engine room beyond the workshop had a far less pleasant smell and occasionally emitted a rivulet of oil to discolour sawdust that looked as beautiful as winnowed corn on our granary floor. I should never have been there but I wandered rather a lot as a child, carried along by the wonder of this thing and then that, the 'whittericks' (stoats) hunting, or partridges running along the grass verge of the dusty farm road.

Our road led to the Hillhead where everything happened. Here the postman sometimes left yesterday's newspaper and our bills and letters. Here the travelling grocer stopped his van to sell loose sugar and other commodities the cottagers needed. Here the traveller, weary of pedalling a bicycle up so many hills, jumped off his machine to pass the time of day and the gossip of the countryside for miles. Here I came to see how the hub of a cartwheel was fashioned from a block of wood, how the segments of it were put together ready for the wheelshod which the smith, who worked a mile or so away, would put on it, cooling the broad 'hoop' with water artfully poured from a can to shrink the iron.

Down at the Hillhead lived old Milligan the shepherd, who never had less than three Border collies about his door, and next to the joiner's cottage lived a relative of his who was a moorland keeper, not only of grouse, but of bees that stored heather honey. Below the joiner's dwelling were the cottages of old Miss Dunbar, the retired schoolmistress who taught me not to take more biscuits from the barrel than my small clenched fist could extract without breaking them, and beyond that the poacher who kept his dog locked up all day and exercised it only at night. That lurcher was something I coveted more than the finest bone-handled knife on display in the saddler's window in town. The clever hound never came out through a hole in the hedge without something in its mouth—a hen pheasant, a rabbit, or a hare.

The joiner himself fascinated me more than anyone, however. I used to think he must have gone to bed with a pipe in his mouth. Like the men who worked in our barn and granary, he smoked a pipe fitted with a little silver cover to prevent sparks escaping and setting fire to the place, but it didn't stop his workshop going up in flames and illuminating the whole countryside one grim day when clouds came in low from the Mull and the Atlantic beyond. The Hillhead on fire advertised itself.

In all the villages for miles old men listened with incredulity to the news and said, 'Damn it, do you tell me that?', and the next day asked the postman what it looked like with the roof fallen in and the old buck engine exposed in a jumble of buckled tin and charred spars. It wasn't long before everything was made good again, however, and the joiner was back in business, making a wheelbarrow for this one, a coffin for that one and milking stools for the byre. Even the sense of drama faded and an engine with a different throb, a more urgent beat, took the place of the one that went for scrap. If the joiner was less free with his tobacco and matches, I never noticed. The pipe always remained part of his physical make-up, but then the fire was probably caused by a spark when the engine backfired and had nothing to do with the joiner's weakness for black twist rubbed in the palm of his hand.

It was the joiner who took me to the river and showed me where the salmon lay. He was probably the best salmon fisherman for twenty or thirty miles, and knew exactly when to go. It was almost certainly the only time he was absent from the Hillhead in all the years he lived there.

The black shed is gone now, alas, and the joiner undoubtedly had his coffin made by someone else. I remember him because like old Miss Dunbar and the blacksmith, he was an important figure in the world of my childhood.

Angling Diversions

An Angler's Confession

When I was less than ten years of age I went into the ironmonger's shop and came out with my first trout flies. They were flies of the type called Bloody Butcher. At the time I didn't know that they were so named because of the bit of red in their make-up.

'Here,' said the ironmonger, 'this fly is a Bloody Butcher.'

How was I to know that he said the words in capital letters? I thought he was strongly recommending a fly that literally butchered the trout. I gasped at the frankness of his description. It made me feel very adult, and, after all, was not the ironmonger one of the stalwarts of the Kirk? Some years later I discovered two other flies called, respectively, the Butcher and the Kingfisher Butcher, and I knew then that the language of fly fishing is colour and poetry. I caught a trout with one of those Bloody Butchers on my cast. It was not my first trout by a few score, but it was my first taken on the fly. I was very proud of that trout, for, having an idea that a fly should skip the water and not be washed away, I dapped the Bloody Butcher along the surface and one of the many trout in the pool was fool enough to come up and hook himself. I think it was that day that the disease took hold, although I didn't begin to fish with intensity until years later.

The blacksmith was to blame for my interest in fishing. He had the gift of persuasion that all anglers have. He could persuade himself and anyone who would listen, talking them into a burning desire to be off up the water. When I think of him now I feel sure he was a relative of Huckleberry Finn. Once I took a mare to be shod and when I reached the smithy rain was dripping gently from the slates of the roof, the fire was low, the coals were black and the anvil silent, for the smith was whipping an ancient rod.

'Now see, boy,' he said. 'I'll put shoon on your horse, but not yet. First I've got to wet the line. The water has colour today. Here, dig me some worms at the midden side.'

I took the fork and dug up as many worms as filled a tin. They were little red worms made by God for the sole purpose of man in catching trout. So the smith said. In a little while we were a mile from the smithy with a dozen trout in the bag, up on the side of the moss where the curlews were nesting and the fresh air of spring rustled in the sleeping heather. Years after, when the thing was in my blood, I longed to catch a dozen fish as handsome as those dark beauties from the shelter of the firs and the moss banks.

My great-uncle farmed near a loch that had been drained for some reason or other and in the cut that ran from the drained loch were scores of fine trout. They were safe in the rocky channel that was overgrown on either side by blackthorn and blackberry, elder and spindle. I used to watch those trout by the hour on sunny days. They ignored the worm I dangled from the stone bridge and the fly I once drifted to them by means of an oak apple and a piece of gut. Perhaps they were there to fire my imagination, to let me see what a hundred big trout looked like when the sun streamed into the clear water of the cut and betrayed each one by his wavering shadow.

When I had finished with school I came north for a holiday and went at the invitation of friends of the family to fish the river I had so often looked at from our own hog-backed hills. A great salmon rose that day, but not to the Logie I had on my cast. I saw a pike caught by a schoolboy, but came home in the gloaming empty-handed, as will anyone who knows nothing of the way of a salmon. I might never have fished again. In all other things a man's unsuccessful first experience is likely to be daunting, but anyone with the poorest ear for poetry will begin to respond again to things that are called by such music as Blae and Black, Teal and Green, Mallard and Claret, Blue Dun, Silver Sedge, Woodcock and Harelug. There is an enchanting thing called a Blue Winged Olive and a score of others named Pale Wateries, Blue Quills, Black Gnats and March Brown Spiders.

One afternoon when I was in London, killing an hour between one appointment and another, I turned off a main thoroughfare and came upon a shop that took me home at once. It was filled with cabinets of the magic flies the ironmonger had sold me. I could gaze at illustrations of solitary men fishing pools in the shadows of tall mountains and wonder at the fascination of feather and silk that was a man-made Olive to float upon the pool as gently as a water spider, as cunningly as the newly hatched fly about to rise and sail into the breeze. A Bloody Butcher sat in a covey of Bloody Butchers, and a Coch-y-Bondhu, the mystery fly of Wales, buzzed like a minute bee beneath its covering of celluloid. While I stood there the curlew called on the moss, the midges danced above the water in the shelter of the firs and the evening sun glinted where the water tumbled through the stones. I could smell peat reek, hear the black-faced sheep bleating, and the roar of the Strand was no more, the red procession of buses at Charing Cross was the dream, and reality was

148

the water flowing over my boots and the whip of the rod in my hand was like some living thing. The door of the shop closed behind me. The little bell stopped tinkling and I felt that I had walked into one of the shops in a village at home.

A seller of flies and rods and reels came forward.

'I'm going fishing again,' I said.

He showed no surprise. This thing happens often. A man becomes a boy again, a boy refuses to become a man. I looked at rods that were made of greenheart and reminded me of old sporting prints. I handled others of split cane, single and double-built, and I began to set myself on fire with thoughts of mountain lakes and singing streams. Back in Wales, where I now live, I carried my gear to a stream that runs through a quiet valley. I lured a trout with a gliding dry fly and snagged another with a sunken Butcher. They were small, stunted little fellows. Sometimes when I caught them in particular places they turned out to have pink flesh. Sometimes they fought with all the vigour of trout twice their size. Sometimes they rose on a glassy lake and took my tiny Blue Quill and delighted my heart. The extraordinary thing was that none was half as big, half as handsome as the fish of the smithy stream, grown more beautiful and twice as large by the passing of years. For some strange reason I did not want them to be, but they were part of another magic that was the flight and call of the sandpiper, the bounce of the dipper, the bobbing of the wagtail.

At times I trudged wearily out of the hills at the end of a warm spring day and encountered other solitary men who carried rods and creels. Once in a while I talked to them. On rare occasions I drank a glass of ale and listened to the story of their affliction. I discovered in the course of this another kind of man, who thought nothing of the hackle and the herl, who saw no beauty in the peacock or the partridge, but had so much of the old hunter in him that his search was for the oldest, the biggest and the most cunning fish that had been locked away in some lonely pool. His consuming fever was to catch the cannibal with the hooked jaw or the pike that rose to take the mallard's brood. He was a man who did what was called spinning, a practice that makes the masters of the dry fly spin in their graves like boxwood tops. This infection took me too. I lost my sleep in spring thinking about the morrow and the rising of a trout to a small dark fly. I lost my sleep in autumn thinking of giant pike sliding through the water to gorge my spinner.

Time is said to heal all things, but nothing heals the disease that gets into the bones and soul of an angler. There is a major conspiracy against his recovery. Once every year his supplier of rods and flies will send him a coloured brochure displaying all the magic that caught him in his callow youth. He will look at the sleek little minnow, the spoon that glints and turns, the diving plug bait, the wobbling imitation of a miller's thumb, or the rainbow colours of lures that catch fictitious fish. Of this afflicted company I have become one. It began, as I have said, a long time ago in a blacksmith's shop where the millrace turned a wheel and the sound of the water was often as loud as the hammer and the quenching iron. In spring my imagination stimulates me to climb for an hour to reach a mountain lake. If it does not, then I am a physically sick man. If November passes and I have not thought of a great green pike, I have not thought at all. There is no cure that is not taken beside the water, among the boulders and in the shade of a tree that rakes the stream, and no cure that lasts more than one setting of the sun.

The Christmas Pike

It began, as adventures begin, with talk that fired both the talker and the listener with an enthusiasm that made nothing of steep hills and cold air, air an overcoat colder than the air of the valley, as people who knew the place vowed. Once or twice as this enthusiasm began to grow I looked at the far-away hills dusted with castor sugar snow. The sky out there was clear of clouds, but the December sun rode in a mellow veil of atmosphere that reminded me of butter muslin. As the talk went on I could hear the whistling wings of duck passing over and see the grouse in the shelter of the peat bank. As I waded down through the round rushes to the lakeside the barren ewes that had been left to graze that poor ground bumped and bounced out of my path. I wanted to catch a pike at Christmas. I wanted a great green fish like a submarine, one that lived away down in the water and watched the surface of the lake so that he could come bursting up to take an unwary duck or moorhen. I wanted a pike that would be hard to catch and I wanted to be out there in that oriental engraving of snowy landscape where the moor runs to the mountains and the high hills seem to hold up the sky.

The water would be dark and cold, we told each other. The thing to do would be to use a heavy spoon and a weight, to fish when the morning sun was across the water and a pike might be moving in search of his prey. We thought of the place in the soft summer evening when rain spattered across the water. We knew the derelict farm that had sheltered us from a thunderstorm and we knew the moorland road and every lonely hilltop and scree of rotten rock. Tomorrow, we said, tomorrow when the sun was hardly lighting the backs of distant hills. We each went home to rummage through a tackle box and inspect rods and reels.

It is hard to explain why I suffer from the excitement of anticipation, a thing that often spoils my shooting. I rarely sleep well on the eve of a day's fishing. The reel screams, the rod bends, the water boils. I fumble with gaff or landing net and run a fever. A whole night such dreams take, a whole night in which fatigue is born of the strain of catching more fish than I may ever live to catch. Down in the lower village cocks began to crow before my mind found peace. They were rusty-throated cocks, scrawny birds whose whole existence was for the purpose of crowing the morning and answering the crowing of their neighbours. I rose and went down to make tea at an hour when only those restless fowls could claim that day was coming. My preparations of the night before left me very little to do. All was ready. I drank my tea and watched the slow-moving clock; and when a little two-stroke motor-bicycle went humming through the village like a bee as it carried its rider to his work in the next county, I gathered my rod and tackle and carried it all with rubber boots and flask and knapsack to the garage.

My companion waited for me with an unshaven face and a restless look in his eye. He, too, thought of the calm water of the lake up there in the sleeping country and the pike to be caught at Christmas.

'We're mad,' he said, and laughed; but his excitement burned.

The journey to the moor is one of twenty-five miles or thereabouts. The road runs over little green hills, along the sides of woods, past snug cottages and clusters of farms. There are several villages on the way. The day was slow in breaking, and we passed through the first village when the windows were lit but the doors closed. We bumped over a hump-backed bridge and sped on by stark willows and leafless hedges. The second village was stirring, and by then daylight was above the elms, touching the smoke from a score of chimneys. The rocks were black ornaments in the tops of the trees and a shaggy pony stood at the gate of a frost-rimed field. In the third village our passing was noted. An old man turned to watch us go, wondering at the sight of our rods and our unkempt appearance as well as our air of urgency; but we were away, uphill out of the chimney smoke and on and on between trees of ash and hedges of hazel, to the stony brows and the rowans, the dead bracken and the shrivelled ling.

At the turn by the first moorland farm we felt the ice on the road. In half a mile we saw the dusting of snow that had fallen on a yellow afternoon when the wind was half north and half east. The fence wires were wrapped in frost. The heather stems were black and the brush silver. We stopped once to examine a glassy hill, and away to our right the morning world was a wonderland of soft sunlight and snowy peaks. The bleating of a sheep came to us across a mile of wild moor in the grip of winter. No grouse called. The world belonged to us from the place in which we stood to the distant shoulder where the road topped the rise and ran on to the first lake. Here on the left they had ploughed the heather with some special kind of plough and had left the great furrows unbroken, and there, by the roadside, a repair gang had left their tool-box until spring came over the moor again.

'The water will be cold,' my companion warned. 'Like lead,' I added; 'but the pike must feed, and cold days follow cold days up here.' We did not need to encourage each other, but it was good to break such silence. At the top of the rise we rounded the shoulder and slowed again. The first lake was in sight. Its reeds were frozen. The water was motionless. It looked as though it might be freezing at that moment: but this was the high lake, this was not our lake. Our lake was comparatively sheltered and even the thicker snow ahead could not daunt us. Our exhilaration was something that those who were beginning the day away out there in the unhealthy smoke of towns, trundling the unfrozen roads in steamed-up buses, could never know.

We hurried on, along the line of the sagging fence, the peat bank and the snow-covered drain, out over the last stretch of flat country before the downhill run to the shelf and the track that branched to our lake. The snow was even thicker on the way down. We sang a Christmas carol until we came to the track and here we stopped, for a drift blocked our way. Twenty miles and more we had come and the lake was less than a mile away. Nothing could stop us now. A drift might stop the car, but we could plough through on foot. We unloaded our gear. A curlew, a lonely bird, went silently over. When he was almost out of sight he still had not called. We looked back after a little while to see the way we had come and then looked forward across the unbroken snow to see the lake. It was a strangely still lake. No breeze stirred the surface. The derelict farm crouched at the far end and on the shoulder above it was the dead tree where a buzzard sometimes perched. No buzzard flew, no ducks were on the water, but all at once the morning sun came over the rim of the moor and blazed like gold on the lake. We struggled hopefully on.

A man of little heart might have blown his hands, taken a drink from his flask and turned about, for the water was so cold that the hungriest pike was surely in the dark caverns of the deep. But we began to put our rods together, struggling to thread the line through the rings, to recover bits of tackle that dropped from numbed fingers and fasten trace to lure and line to trace. There is something about fishing that calls for extraordinary faith, faith in the day, in the colour of the water, the turn of the spoon, the spinning of a minnow, and we had, above all else, a great faith. At the first cast or two the line began to freeze in the top rings of the rod, but we cast again and again. The sun glared on the crystalline snow and flashed on the water. An impudent perch took my spoon and raised my hopes, but he was a misguided little creature come up from the foot of the rocks on which I stood. No other fish came to do as he had done. No pike rushed after the lure and turned like a snake, green and fierce-snouted as some prehistoric monster. The sun continued to shine and the air grew colder and I thought of Christmas a day or two away, Christmas as crisp and clear as a Christmas card painting, a dead tree, sun on the snow-covered banks and one solitary water bird, a grebe, I think it was, that came and settled out there on the water, turning and paddling about, a lost creature out of the winter sky.

It was close to noon when the pike rose. My companion and I stood close together, our breath steaming, our hands stiff with cold. Neither of us spoke, but I raised my arm and pointed, forgetting to breathe, almost unable to believe my eyes. He rose as he had done in our imagination. A little wave ran at his passing. He turned and was gone. The wave ran out, smoothing into the water and vanishing until it was hard to be sure that any such thing had really taken place. For a moment we stood still, staring at where he had risen, and then we began to cast again and again until we had covered the area a score of times and tired our arms, but it had happened and it was over. The sun slid into the butter muslin haze, a little wind made a snow flurry rise from the drifts. The dead tree looked more gaunt and the lake frowned as the breeze passed over its surface. The Christmas pike had fed. He might brood down there for a week, a month, perhaps longer. How often does a fish feed in cold weather? Who can tell?

On our way home we stopped at one of the village inns. Two old men inspected us with great curiosity. A pike out of the lake at Christmas? It was a dream. No pike fed in that place between November and April and if we had seen one rise we had taken ale before setting out. We nodded a little sadly. Perhaps we had taken a sort of ale, the wine of adventure, the intoxicating brew of enthusiasm. Our faces were snow-burnt, our blood a-tingle and we had been up there on the silent moorland road where the curlew passed over without calling and everything was in the hand of winter. We consoled ourselves with an odd contradiction of the thing that had made us set out at cock-crow. It was plain that what we had seen had been some sort of magic pike. The pike of October, the pike of July and the hungry fish of August slept down in the bottom of the lake, hibernating like hedgehogs. Sometimes a foolish perch came up to look at the winter sun, but no pike rose at Christmas, except a dream creature, as big as a dog, as fierce as a plunging eagle, and this monster—twice as big as any fish anyone had ever taken—showed itself only to those who reached the place in a golden sunlight when the snow sparkled and the lake was still. We had seen what no one else had seen, a magic Christmas pike, as uncatchable as a snowflake.

Gone Upstream

If I'm not at home and my rod is missing, you can take it that I've gone fishing. You might be able to take out a map and make a guess as to which stream or lake I've chosen. It will be a mountain stream or a lake in the hills, somewhere quiet, peaceful and perhaps a little remote. At the outset I should make it plain that I'm not a highly-skilled fly fisherman. I count my fish in single units because they sound more that way. I never catch two brace. I catch four fish. I have never fished a chalk stream or used the mayfly in the duffer's fortnight. I was born within reach of moorland water, peaty water tumbling through boulders where heather grew, fir-shaded pools and dark glides between one cascade and the next. It was natural that when I came to live in Wales and looked about for a bit of fishing, I turned to the hill streams and the lakes and pools—the fynnon as they are known in Welsh—the wells and springs that lie in the hills.

I served my apprenticeship to this sort of fishing using the dry fly more often than the wet because I have never managed to become very expert at casting a straight line, although I can throw a good question mark to avoid drag on the floating fly. It is right to tempt small fish with a small fly. Whatever legends are told about big lake trout there are a thousand small ones for every good fish, and the good fish has his day for rising and keeps three hundred and sixty-four for contemplation. A fine cast and a dainty lure represent true art in fly fishing.

Anyone can catch fingerlings, of course, but the mountain stream and lake trout are not fingerlings in the sense that they are undiscriminating. The water in which they live is usually acid and almost sterile, but the fish are mature. If they feed more often than fish in good water—and I am not sure that they do—it is because food is scarce and they cannot afford to let it drift past. Nevertheless, they know what they like. They will take a neat little Blue Quill, a dainty Greenwell or a Coch-y-Bondhu no bigger than an elderberry half grown. In the smooth little basins in the hillside the fur and feather fly must fall softly and sail without drag or line-shadow, as free and innocent as the seed of a weed drifting on the water. The splash of the rise of a mountain trout that takes the fly has the joy of summer in it. The crystal brilliance of beads of water thrown into the sunlight has beauty meant for the eye of a painter or a poet. Once in a while the line must run, the green and yellow, red-spotted trout must turn over and come into the net, but it does not matter whether one puts two fish into the creel in a day or a dozen.

Of my days wandering with a rod I cherish one above all others. I brought home only two fish, but it was a day of enchantment when I came near to being a true angler, and the memory of it lives with me like a pleasant dream. We were to have met in the village that sits under the mountain. It was to have been as soon as the first bus could bring my friend to the place and as soon as I could get there on an ancient bicycle. Transport was a major problem for me at that time, but I had a boundless enthusiasm. Fourteen miles in the brightening light of a summer's morning, a morning when the shadows in the fir woods were blue and the pigeons had begun their love-making, raised my spirits. I reached the little bridge at the end of the village and stood looking at the water while I waited for the sound of the bus, a sleepy bus out of a half-awake town 20 miles away. Two or three small trout rose beneath the bridge, making rings that the fast-flowing stream quickly erased. The sun was not yet on the water, and I couldn't see the fish, but I knew exactly where they were lying. They rose regularly and while I watched their rings the village along the stony street began to awaken, lit its fires, clumped its doors open and shut, whisked a broom across its hearths and put an old dog out to stalk stiffly about until the flags became warm enough for him to lie down.

In the distance I could hear the clatter and rumble of a milk lorry. When it had gone crashing through the village and had taken its jangling load into some by-way, I heard the bus. It was exactly ten minutes late. I turned my back on the stream and the little trout and waited. The bus came to a stop. A man in earth-stained corduroys got down and a girl

155

bustled from a cottage and climbed aboard. My friend failed to appear. The next bus was two or three hours away. I hitched my bag on my shoulder, turned into the lane that flanked the stream and plodded uphill, brushing a cobweb from my face and noticing that above the water and close beneath the overhanging hazels a little company of midges had started to dance like tiny flecks of ash above a hot fire. At the first level run of water I left the lane and went to the stream to put up my rod and tie on my fly.

Before I moved away I sat down and took a page from my diary and wrote on it the words, 'Gone Upstream,' then placed the piece of paper on a boulder with a pebble to hold it down. My friend, if he came at last, would know that I had arrived and, perhaps, hurry up to join me.

I fished my way up water, taking two small trout and putting them back, watching the dipper and a snail on a stalk, until I came to the first pool, an excavation at the mouth of an old lead mine. The underwater was white with quartz rubble and the bowl of the pool was green with trailing weed and moss-capped boulders. From one side it was possible to approach the water and make a cast, but on the other side the bank towered like a miniature cliff. It was a formidable task to get a line across the pool, but in the side of the little cliff three trout rose one after the other, taking flies that came down and swirled to them as a small waterfall spent its force. I sat a while pondering this thing.

The midges rose, the water sang and time passed. I made a score of attempts, and the Blue Quill still fell short and failed to get across the current to the eddy below the high bank. When I looked at my watch it was well past noon. I had been more than three hours trying my hand, slipping on green rocks and risking my neck above a deep hole among submerged rocks. The sun moved and struck down through the trees so that I could see my three dark trout. Each one looked more than a pound in weight and each was probably a little less than half a pound. I wandered round the pool and perched myself above them, sitting on the fine short grass and watching how they rose and settled after every morsel that passed. While I was there an oak apple came bobbing and swinging along out of the fall.

I began to think of the oak gall and my fine cast. I had my lunch before I went in search of an oak. Have you ever tried to find an oak apple in summer? For some reason they are not easy to come by. It took me an hour to find an oak stalk to which three hard galls still adhered. I fastened one of them to my cast and went back to the fall, drew line off my reel, flicked the gall and my fly—a well-oiled fly—into the stream and let the pull of the gall and the current take my line away. The fly sailed out of the fall and trailed in the eddy, while the gall sailed closer to the middle of the pool. The first trout rose. I saw him open his mouth and turn as he took my Blue Quill, and then I walked him down the pool to the place where the stream ran out. He was not a pound in weight, but he was a stout little fish and I was not ashamed to put him in my bag.

About an hour later, the remaining fish began to feed again. I lost the second when he had taken my fly and he went off to sulk in deeper water. The third trout moved up and began to feed where the first had had his station. The Blue Quill came out of the fall looking so like a struggling insect that I was almost deceived myself. At the tail of the pool I lifted the fish and laid it with its brother. It had taken me more than nine hours to put two fish in the bag, but when I turned and went down water I was content.

The note on the stone had been moved. I picked it up. It read, 'Missed you somewhere. Gone to catch the bus.' My friend had taken a short cut to get upstream quickly and had passed me there in the first pool, playing for my two dark trout like a schoolboy after tadpoles or minnows. I smiled and scratched my midge-bites as I rode home.

Short Cuts to a Full Creel

The old keeper who managed the boat for us on the loch last summer was a man of great experience in many arts. For instance, he knew how to grow plums better than the head gardener on the estate on which he had worked for many years. He knew the ways of wild cats. He was an expert in preparing a salmon for shipment and insisted on taking me away down to the reed-bed, watching him cut reeds and making a cover for the fish I was to take home by car the next day. He also knew how to manage a drift and what were the best and most productive parts of the best bays on the right side of the loch. He was also a master of the gentle art of fishing the gentle or maggot. That was one of the secrets he imparted in a whisper.

Maggot-fishing wasn't controlled. It just wasn't done—officially. It wasn't talked about. The subject came up only because we had decided to fish the evening rise on that very dour water, and to come off able to hold up our heads we had to have something more than a wet fly and a lot of faith, he said. I am not a purist. I never have been. I have fished the dry fly for the greater part of my fishing life not because I see some particular virtue in the method but because it has provided me with the greatest delight.

The wet fly is an equally great art. It requires greater patience and perhaps more imagination. I would never quarrel about the merits of one or the other of the two schools of fly-fishing. The maggot, now, is something different. It has its advocates for certain purposes and under certain circumstances. It is the sea trout angler's stand-by, and he needs no great excuse, because his fly is more often than not a lure, and the maggot bridges the gap between bait and lure.

Walton included the gentle, beloved, he said, by the anglers of the south, as a fitting bait for the roach, rudd, dace and so on. He didn't include it in his baits for trout, because, I think, it had never struck him to try. He listed some flies of doubtful entomology, but he wasn't an ethical fly-fisherman or any sort of purist. He was an angler after fishes, dallying by the river or stream to take a chub, a carp, perch or pike by whatever means would serve. He strained his imagination to improve the armoury of every devotee of the varied branches of angling without saying: 'Do you fasten upon your hook, dressed in the manner of a fly, a gentle or maggot, for this you will quickly discover is something trouts are partial too, particularly in places where streams or rivers enter lakes, and often as the sun goes off the water.' Walton didn't say that, and nor did Francis Francis in his turn, although he had given the maggot some thought. He urged the angler who went after grayling to try the maggot because the grayling came quickly to its movement. It improved the fly. It filled the bag.

Without humbug, one may acknowledge the maggot for what it is—a stage between imitation of the natural fly and the natural fly itself. Trout have been offered maggots for a long, long time. When I was a boy the envious would look at a newly-caught trout of exceptional size and name the fly without waiting to be told—the maggot fly. The indignation that resulted from such an accusation was often a guide to the true facts. The maggot was fished when the maggot could be readily found.

There were alternatives, of course. The maggot itself could be imitated, but then so could a fly. Imitating the maggot with wool and silks was not much to the liking of those who couldn't tie flies. Their remedy was to peel the skin from a round rush and use the pith, which has the same colour as a maggot. A less effective imitation was a small piece of chamois leather, carefully cut, impaled on the hook of a fly such as the Butcher or Peter Ross. Both had drawbacks, for the maggot requires the same thing as the bloodworm needs to lure a fish— movement, life and, perhaps, flavour.

158

That the maggot is being used more and more intensively in public waters, and furtively on strictly controlled streams and lakes, I have no doubt. People who know tell me that its advance has come about through the improvement in road transport. Skilled match fishermen from the south have adventured into more remote places in the north and shown the locals what they already knew but didn't apply. Even the trout that hasn't seen a blowfly maggot quickly learns that it is a tasty morsel. Match fishermen use liberal quantities of maggots to bait a swim on occasions. Trout can be as easily persuaded to feed in a place where maggots are scattered as they can to take chopped liver, and the maggot on the fly is the frustrated trout fisherman's compromise with his conscience.

Less and less do the fishermen who once put on a maggot at dusk go in search of the carrion's food. They know that they can buy a tin of prime, liver-fed maggots, coloured or uncoloured, simply by putting in an order for them. It is hard to say that they lack a philosophy so far as sport is concerned. They attend upon the trout to catch them, and the maggot makes things much more certain.

The old keeper who led me to fish the rise with maggot on the fly smiled as he produced the jar. Sausages, he called them and, although we were perhaps half a mile from the landing-stage and the dusk was settling, he still whispered. I put a maggot on each fly and fished it, and the trout rose; and we caught enough to save our blushes, providing no one examined us in the lamplight. I found myself thinking that after all, there is a certain skill in trolling, spinning and the like, and who could really tell whether the trout rose to the fly or the maggot? One thing about dry-fly fishing is that the fly must float. It won't support the weight of a wriggling maggot. I don't have to try to know that, and there is something to be said for trying anything practicable at least once—the maggot on the wet fly, the gentle art.

Fishing in the Land of Haunted Waters

The main tourist attraction of Wales is the aspect of its mountains, and where there are mountains there are turbulent streams, and rivers and lakes. There are so many rivers and lakes in Wales that few anglers, if any, can ever claim that they have fished in all of them, although the country is small. I remember once flying high over the Welsh coast and seeing the pattern of mountain, moorland and sparkling waters laid out before me in the morning light. I was fascinated, for this fed the romantic dream I had always cherished as an angler—a belief that if I had an endless summer I could move on, discovering yet another secret water, another llyn at the head of another cwm, for as long as I cared to journey.

By comparison with the fishing lakes of Ireland, or the wild waters of the highlands of Scotland, the lakes of Wales might be described as a Lilliput collection, particularly if one excepts Bala, sometimes called Llyn Tegid, Vrynwy and one or two others that are known to the tourist because of their easy access. The majority of the waters that really lure the dedicated angler into the secret and lonely places have to be sought as diligently as the end of the rainbow, and once one begins this exploration it is likely to become an obsession, for there is always another little stretch of water beyond the next ridge, across the shoulder of the mountain up on the plateau and facing the morning sun.

There is a mystery, a fascination that the angler soon learns is best appreciated without guidance or advice. True, some of the more enchanting places where he casts his line may turn out to be polluted, or contaminated by the residue of ancient copper washings or rubble from lead mines, but disappointments of this sort are offset on other occasions. In my own case I remember having to climb to a ridge that was over 2,000 feet, on the way to a remote lake, which turned out to be quite barren, but just below the ridge I stopped to cast a fly in a little green pool that reflected the white clouds of the summer sky, and there to my astonishment I picked up a golden trout that weighed over three-quarters of a pound and took a dry fly as neatly as any chalk-stream giant.

Nearly all the Welsh lakes, large or small, have a wild beauty that delights the visitor, even when he catches only small trout, as he will in most of them; but some of the more remote waters, dour though they may be, contain a few big trout to provide excitement for the angler who goes there on the right day. A sort of prospector's fever comes upon the man who fishes these hill tarns, knowing that a combination of sun and cloud and just the right temperature may give him the chance of a fish that a dozen visitors have never had. The tourist, unfortunately, can hardly compare his chances with those who live in the mountains. He must go when he can and where he can, having taken advice; but the tourist who comes more than once in a season quickly learns that the easily-reached waters contain mostly small trout or no trout at all,

unless, of course, they are preserved and private. To prove that the Welsh lake or river can support as fine and handsome a fish as ever sheltered in the trailing weed of a chalk stream, the diligent fly-fisherman will occasionally take a fish of two or three pounds from a ticket water. Before he has fished two or three seasons in the land of the cwms and peaks he will learn of fish of five or six pounds caught a season back on a Coch-y-Bonddu or a Black Gnat; a season back, because those who found this water kept quiet, and now things are harder than they were. He will see photographs of these fish. They are not figments of the imagination, and he will, if he is lucky, see or be given one or two of the rough local flies on which the monsters were taken. The flies will strike him as being somewhat large, and he will doubt his ability to fish such lures with confidence; but if he cultivates the friendship of the more expert locals he will discover the technique. If he fishes a lifetime he will catch his share in this valley, the next, or the one beyond the misty skyline.

Having lived a good part of my life in Wales, I would say that it is not the country for a fish-hungry angler anxious to escape his frustration and lay a fine catch on a salver every evening. It is rather the country for the dedicated fisherman, who loves the atmosphere of the plunging torrent, the river rising fast and the fish ploughing through from one pool to the next, the brooding tarn and soft green of the mountain reflected in the depths. It takes time to discover the places, and they vary from one season to another. Lakes come into condition and provide wonderful fishing for a short time and then fall back, perhaps for five or six years. It takes time to explore, and in time one learns that all of these waters have names whether the map indicates the fact or not. The poetry of Welsh names is nowhere better than in the description of the lakes and pools, and when the angler sits on a boulder, wondering about the time of the rise, if any, he may contemplate that this crystal-clear strip of water is the lake of the bird, or the servant's well. Away in the mist below the peaks are the lakes of the hound, across the valley lies the lake of the water dragon, the spring of the frog, the Sunday well. The old men of the village tell of good trout in the lake of the red rock or the black pool.

How can a visitor discover where to fish in Wales? There are a few guides. None of them, I would say, particularly reliable or up to date, save in details of licences and ticket charges. Information is scant and hard to come by, because the best fishing is rather like Welsh gold. A large number of anglers come to Wales lured by a description of fishing that, to say the least, is somewhat coloured by imagination. It is easier for some people to catch a tourist than to demonstrate the catching of a good trout, and the best description of the Welsh lakes is long out-dated. It was compiled by Frank Ward, who, 30 years ago, wrote *The Fishing Lakes of Wales*. No one has yet seen fit to retrace the steps of this grand old angler, a kindly man whom I once met while fishing on Anglesey. Perhaps no one has been quite as inspired as he was. He laid no claim to great skill, although his talent was considerable and his book was produced with the unselfish purpose of guiding others through the great pattern of the little-known waters of Wales. In the course of his investigations Frank Ward noted every water that the large-scale map included and marked down whether permission could be obtained to fish there, who the owner was, the sort of fish the water held, the best shore to fish, the most favourable wind, and often the likely fly. The legends were included because nearly every water in Wales is haunted, contains a water stallion, a dragon, a ghost. The book is long out of print, and anyone who takes it as a guide now must expect to be disappointed in many places. Yet it is something to have as a rough guide, for it tells the angler where there are no fish, where the fish are small, where the banks are dangerous, and so on, and it covers the whole of Wales. Ward had George Borrow's feeling for the out-of-the-way places, and one day someone may yet fish in as many Welsh lakes as he did, and bring everything up to date.

At different times I have fished for nearly all the sorts of fish to be caught in Wales with the exception of char, gwyniad, bream and carp; but it is, of course, a country of game fish, of salmon, sea trout and brown trout. For some people, delight lies in the valley, where they devote themselves to intercepting the running fish; for others, and not by any means the under-privileged, the real mystery and wonder lie in the deep water of the mountain lakes, something, I fear, beyond my powers of description but understood by kindred spirits, who ask for no more.

Crepuscular Ways of the Sea Trout

It is sometimes said that man and his persistent fowling through the centuries have slowly and steadily induced duck to feed by night and fly upriver, and to and from the marsh, in the twilight. Whether this is the real truth of the matter or not, it seems to me almost as logical to suggest that the crepuscular behaviour of the sea trout might also be laid at man's door. The sea trout is taken by day, of course, and by every means that may be applied by night, the use of bait as well as the fly; but the nocturnal behaviour of the migratory trout goes a little beyond the depredations of the predatory angler.

Time and again the sea trout comes upriver, splashing, wriggling and working his way frantically on his side to pass from a shallow run to a deeper pool. He can be seen, once he has struggled on his side to water in which he can only just swim, making a long wake as he hurries on to safer runs. On the way he might be intercepted by man, or mutilated, if not destroyed, by the fishing heron, the otter and even the black-backed gull, did he not choose the twilight to move on, rising to the moth or whatever creature similar to his seafood he may encounter beyond the salt. Heron and otter may move in the sheltering shadows of gathering dusk.

The sea trout fisherman who fishes by night does so because he has studied the business, or follows in the footsteps of the expert. It is not a convention that makes the salmon fisherman think about sea trout when the light goes. He may, of course, take his salmon after night falls, but not with any certainty—not without a greater degree of luck than he already prays for when he spins, or uses the fly or any of the less conventional lures employed to take a salmon. The salmon is for the day. The sea trout's world is the world of shadow—brooding willows, inky blackness below the elms, grotesque outlines on the riverside hillocks, and the river endlessly talking to itself as it flows over and round boulders and sweeps along the undercut bank.

Flies for sea trout are generally a good deal larger than those employed for the brown trout, his anchorite relative living a lifetime in one pool and growing only as big as the food of the river permits. The sea trout's virility, condition and silvery brilliance are the product of life in the sea. When he comes back he takes a fly that looks something like the fry to which he has been accustomed in salt water or the estuary. He lived on shrimp, prawn and sand eel for the important period of his development. Once he was no better than the fingerling brown, but he comes back to the river to spawn, strong and eager to get far upstream. In the early days of his conditioning to the change he takes lures that resemble the whitebait and the sand eels. The fresh water may ultimately sicken him, and he may spend days and nights splashing in the pools, slapping himself down on the surface for no reason at all.

The sea trout enthusiast hopes for a fresh run of fish. The passing of days, the change of temperature and perhaps a general sickness or shrinking of his stomach through unaccustomed hunger in less fertile water, make the handsome fish from the sea untakeable to all but the wiliest of sea trout anglers—those who have a trick or two up their sleeves and use wake-producing lures. The sea trout follows the V of water or the ripple produced by drawing any reasonable wake-producing object across the pool; but here again the angler who is most skilled knows that the half light at least is essential, and darkness aids him most.

What the sea trout sees on different nights and how it will react from hour to hour between dusk and dawn is part of the great mystery surrounding migratory fish in general and the reason why they rise, or turn to things cast to them. A brown trout rises to insects that sail on the surface or to hatching nymphs. Cast a dry fly in the dark, and, if it happens to be big enough and creates enough disturbance as it swings along at the end of the cast, it may be taken equally well by the sea trout or the night-feeding big brown trout. Sea trout and the salmon are more generally found in comparatively barren pastures, and fishing for brown trout by night is a little beyond the pale. After all the brown trout is always there. He can be tackled at leisure one day in May or June. He can be lured with the mayfly or the lesser ephemeridae. The sea trout does not promise to stay. If he stays in the pool, he is likely to become almost as sullen as the old red salmon with the ugly kelp. He must be met at his favoured time—in the night, an hour or two before midnight, perhaps, the hour when dawn is being heralded by the slow movement of cloud towards the west and the combing out of the eastern darkness.

Sea trout anglers, it always seems to me, are men with uncomfortable beds and incredible single-mindedness, at least those worthy of the name—the sort who see the light fade and are still there to hear the dog bark at dawn. Who else but the fanatic would haunt the river for an unbroken seven or eight hours' fishing?

The sea trout reacts to the slightest change in barometric pressure. Some say that he may begin to move when, miles down river, the tide begins to run again. If the persistent angler, casting his line across and down the water without intermission for the first three hours of the night, does not feel a plucking at the fly, or have it taken with the violence the hungry fresh-run fish may display, then he shrugs his shoulders and waits, fishing as steadily as ever, changing the lure once or twice from the Teal, Silver and Blue, to some more exotic thing dressed with peacock harl and more liberally armed with hooks. When the tide backs up in the faraway estuary the migratory trout may begin to rise. If this does not happen, it remains to fish the hour or two before dawn, so long as the mist does not roll through the water meadows and hide the looming shadows of the pollard willows and the sentinel oaks beyond. When mist crawls along the river and the line vanishes in the milky nothingness above the water, even the fanatic reels in and goes sadly away.

What is it all for? Pot-hunters would say it is for a fish that weighs perhaps ¾ lb. but might go up to 20 lb., and has the most delicate, the finest flavour of any sort of fish caught in the river or the sea. The others, who have used all the lures and techniques ever described in angling handbooks, who have been gnawed and irritated to distraction by the swarming midges and have gone in over their thighboots time and again, say it is strictly a business for the mentally deranged.

A Good Day for Trout

The time was when I awoke even before first light to listen for the wind and the rain, and wondered whether it would be a good day up in the hills. There is nothing that produces greater frustration in this business of fly-fishing than the weather. One can cope with a tangled cast, a sinking line or the preference of the rising fish for everything but the fly one casts to them, but the weather makes or mars the day completely, and it may change in an hour or two. Nothing has gone out of fly-fishing so far as I am concerned. I am still inwardly excited to see a fish rising or to contemplate a day's fishing. I am a slower starter, that is all.

The trouble is the fishing is not on my doorstep. I must travel from 15 to 40 miles. In one direction the journey is through mountains and in the other across comparatively flat country. In the mountains the weather changes quickly and is often quite different from that prevailing at home before I depart. Across the flatter country the wind is likely to blow with greater force because there are no major windbreaks. Almost always I leave home with my fingers crossed concerning fishing conditions when the time comes to put up the rod. As I drive I wonder whether I shall be wading or making a drift in the boat. Only rarely do my imagination and enthusiasm run riot to the extent that I begin to think of red-letter days and see myself taking the limit imposed on the club water. This once happened, if not in fact, then in theory.

The wind was setting the tops of our pine trees gently swaying. I could imagine the line of broken water on the far bank of the lake and the foam accumulating in creamy clumps among the stones. The sun was bright, but enough fast-moving white clouds passed over. This kept me hoping that there would be moments when brown trout or sea trout might come to the fly without being put off by the polish of the nylon cast brilliantly reflecting the light, or those rope-thick shadows that cast and line make on the bottom when the sun penetrates the water right down to the rising weed. It is better to travel hopefully than to arrive, they say, and if this is a worn cliché, it is nonetheless true. I travelled most hopefully because it seemed that the wind was abating and a barrier of cloud was building up in the south-west. The foam would crumble and the froth wash off the stones, the breakers smooth into a swell and the swell give place to an even ripple. The bite of the wind would give place to a soft moistness and encourage a rising of nymphs in those brief intervals when the sun reflected on the ripple.

Only one boat was on the lake when I reached it. Two or three solitary, heron-like anglers stood plying their rods and working their sunken flies at stations along the uneven bank. The wind had not abated at all. The foam was on the far shore and the breakers showed with depressing regularity. The choice of the day was whether to wade and fish, and use no energy in rowing a boat, or to row and drift and cover as much water as possible. Quite plainly the solitary anglers indicated, by their lack of movement, that they were out of luck. For them one spot was as good as the next. I called on the bailiff and received the rowlocks. The die was cast. Rowing in a wind takes a certain amount of calorific energy and every drift in a strong wind inevitably means a stiff row back in order to start over again.

I began drifting shortly after I had left the mooring, taking the line of least resistance, knowing well that soon I would be rowing right down the lake without the benefit of the shelter provided above the mooring by a belt of larches. No fish rose to the fly, but twice a small sea trout jumped clear of the water. I cannot exactly say why, but I am never encouraged by the sight of fish jumping right out of the water when it is rough. Perhaps it is because I imagine the bottom to be stirred up and muddy in places and the fish, half suffocated after grubbing about in the depths, have to take neat air. On hot days I am sure they jump clear because too much oxygen has been extracted by the blazing sun. On this particular water the jumping fish always seem to be sea trouts or smolts, but, of course, it is hard to identify a bright, healthy young brown trout from a sea trout in a brief moment when they leap and drop back into the waves. My short drift ended almost in the stones. The breakers threatened to lap over the broadsided boat, and I wound in, unshipped the oars and pulled away only just in time.

I had company on the way back, a string of three coots that swam and paddled through the rough, 20 yards to my left. A swan drifted down with her neck folded in the shelter of her wings and her head on her breast, quite careless of the fact that her feathers were being unmercifully ruffled. A little later she came to and turned into the wind, flapped her wings and paddled herself into a sort of water-beating flight that took her back up the lake a great deal faster than I could propel the boat. The coots made no attempt to copy her, but they slowly gained on me. It took me half an hour to win the top end of the lake where the river runs out and the sea trout find entry to pass right through to the other end, finding the river once again. The sea trout, say the experts, follow the course of the river through the lake. There is no map. One should take note of the best place and build up a picture of the river winding from one end of the lake to the other. The brown trout are fonder of the weedier, and perhaps slightly warmer, expanses of water. The sea trout, like the great company of swallows and swifts, are migrants, coming up to spawn and going down to the sea again.

Half an hour to row and perhaps an hour and a half with a dragging anchor to drift down again; three drifts and, late in the day, I found myself among sea trout eager to seize the Peter Ross. Without the long-handled 18-inch net I could not have subdued them or boated one of them. As it was, I came close to the limit of eight, losing half. Perhaps I had spent too much of my strength in unprofitable drifting and rowing, and had I conserved my energy I might have stayed the course to fill my bag with twice as many handsome fish.

Secrets of the Early Lakes

They say that the dedicated fisherman fishes steadily through the season and then spends the whole winter thinking about the next, and there is some truth in this. In Wales the incurable addicts talk and think fishing, and so keenly do some of them anticipate the coming of a new season that they are out in February looking at the water, testing the wind on their cheeks and eagerly trying to detect a softening of the weather for the onset of March. No heron or cormorant was ever more devoted to the pursuit of fishing than some of these fanatics, and it is an odd thing that many of them are men of advanced years, well past the flush of mere amateur or novice enthusiasm.

As everywhere in the British Isles, in Wales there are early lakes and lakes slow to come into fishing condition. The secret of the early lakes is shrouded in mystery. They are, in a way, like mushroom fields, being places to which the initiated hastens before the ordinary angler is properly out of hibernation, for here the early-comer may cast a fly, even when his rod rings are in danger of icing up, and yet hook an eager trout that will dive back into the warmer depths, making the line cut water like a cheese-wire.

It has long seemed to me that the more aesthetic an angler becomes in his approach the less he fishes in hard conditions, for imagination replaces the need for simple physical experience. Ultimately this fisherman goes only on those rare days when the lake presents a picture-book scene, when dream and reality are closest, the soft summer breeze carries a dancing fly over the water and the trout rises to throw jewels of water into the air as it takes the morsel. Things have come near to a sort of Nirvana, and in a few seasons the philosopher may stay at home and dream, fishing no more, a mystic in every sense. There are times when I have an uneasy feeling that this may happen to me, for although I know the early lakes, and the hills draw me as winter leaves the higher slopes, I tend to put off my excursions until May and June.

I console myself with the theory that plump bright trout to test my skill will be more worthy of the encounter when summer is advanced. In high summer the flocks are grazing far into the hills, the ring ouzel is nesting, and sandpipers are chasing one another across the water as the olives are hatching, while in spring the grim face of winter still haunts the high lakes. Early in the season grass and round rushes are bleached, and there are blots of snow in the northerly depression, sheaths of ice on streams that run in gullies.

The early lakes are listed in one's diary, or so well-known that one doesn't need to commit their names to paper; but exactly when the earliest of them becomes fishable depends on the weather.

One must make the journey, because fish know nothing of the calendar. They react in certain ways because of temperature, light, the supply of food in one form or another, and the depth at which they live. If the early lake is slow to turn over, it doesn't follow that the late one will be correspondingly later: yet a late lake is one where the fish remain apparently comatose, while an early one is a water that reveals signs of movement as the days lengthen, and down in the riverside meadows the plovers are nesting.

I know half-a-dozen lakes where there are sizeable trout—and one or two of glasscase proportions—where a fisherman must go in the earliest days of April, if he is to do well, and some where March, in certain seasons, is the best month of all. Some of these lakes are those that later fill with weed. The secret of such places lies, no doubt, in a shallowness that permits an early warming-up of the water, a decided fertility as far as insects and crustaceans are concerned. The mystery of the early lake that has no bays of weed or rich harvest of early hatching flies is something different and more microscopic perhaps—organisms that, although minute, provide the vital constituents for early recovery after the barren days of winter and the spawning at the close of the previous season.

The angler who looks for scientific explanations may consider the whole story of the trout's existence from one season to the next. If he does, somewhere along the line he will decide that he can take well-nourished, fighting trout in June and spare himself the hazard of cold winds and fleeting noon sunlight without a suggestion of warmth. The early lake may not give up its fish in May or June, but in those months the fish will make growth, and the diehards know the sort of trout the otherwise unfishable early lake may yield. The best of the season has passed by June in certain places, and he who fishes only in the warm months misses half the joy of fishing.

To know the early lake is not to have the answer to everything. A cold day in spring is often a step back into winter, and the early lakes are rarely situated in low ground. They are almost invariably waters exposed to more light than sheltered to any great degree. Trout, I think, react to improving light and the blessing of spring sunshine. A water

169

sheltered from the north-east and yet open to as much as possible of the sun's light from morning until late afternoon is likely to be an early one, provided, of course, that it is not of exceptional depth. The secret lies also to some degree in a certain balance of air and water temperature.

Let the faddist take a thermometer in his hand and a barometer on his back; but the practical lake fisherman testing his early-fishing haunt gauges the degree of coldness in the wind and tests the water as he wades from one rock perch to the next. It isn't an exact science, this lake fishing. One must have an instinct for the successful technique and for the conditions that make an early lake what it is. The rise is of short duration, if it is apparent on the surface at all, and it will often be less than an hour from the first suggestion of a touch at the sunken fly, until the place broods and all is over for the day.

There have been many opening days when I took trout and went on to experience blank days in May and June. More than once I have taken trout on the dry fly in March at altitudes of up to 1,800 feet and walked home past lower waters fringed with ice, and many seasons I abandoned my intention to fish a certain little lake high in the mountains, because I had missed the best days in March. In this particular strip of water I had once seen 16 trout of near a pound in weight taken by two anglers on a day when snow was falling and the peaks of Snowdonia obscured in a near-blizzard, and they were fine, fat trout of beautiful colour. A week before I had painstakingly cast and cast again on a much lower lake in which no trout moved, and would not move, I discovered, for at least two months.

Scientists may probe these mysteries and produce papers explaining how they analysed the water, took temperatures at different depths and used seine nets and sampling equipment to investigate the food of the fish; but the dedicated angler will spend only a little time relating such findings to his experience. The early lakes were found by instinct and trial, and the word was passed on. The instinct, which is something like that of the old prospectors who took lead or copper from the hills, might enable the men who possess or acquire it to find similar waters in other places, but it is something they never consider. It has the important and overshadowing end-product—a taste of success at the beginning of the season, proof that the hand hasn't lost its cunning, nor the great mystery its deep and lasting fascination.

Let the dilettante fish only in the days of the fly-fisherman's carnival: the man who fishes when and where he can, and takes his trout in rain or sunshine, is a master angler.

The Salmon's War of Wits

No one can hope to become an expert fisherman unless he makes a careful study of the fish he hopes to catch, a prolonged study that continues so long as he fishes. I remember an old and celebrated salmon fisherman who fished one of the rivers in my part of the world. His name was a byword among salmon fishermen. Some of them were completely overawed by his reputation and a few hinted that no one could be quite so skilled as he seemed to be. He must also be a poacher with some trick up his sleeve, they said, because he caught salmon in spite of the fish and its behaviour. I think they were not only accusing him of poaching but of being a wizard. The old man died and out they came with their favourite story. He could catch a salmon with bait or spinner, fly or lure. He could catch them with a worm and he could catch them without a worm, for once he had stood above a weir and caught salmon with a maggot on a hook, using the maggot as a 'sighter' when he foul-hooked a fish. Mind you, he foul-hooked them so well that you thought the fish had taken it.

All of this was the biggest lot of nonsense. He didn't fish a maggot. He could make a salmon take a worm when it was in the mood to take, and he only fished when he knew what the salmon were likely to be doing. Apart from this he knew exactly where the fish were lying. He could have brought them out of a pool of ink, fishing at precisely the right depth in precisely the right place and with the right retrieve. He had studied salmon as a shepherd studies sheep or a keeper knows the ways of birds, and if he couldn't impart the knowledge to anyone else it was because there was so much of it that had gone down into the subconscious that it could never come out in words. It was an instinct for the ways of the fish.

The average, not very skilled angler tests his instinct every time he goes to the river. When it is good he is elated, even conceited about his success. When it is bad he curses the fish for being fickle and unpredictable. Once in a while he compares one experience with another and comes to a conclusion. Once in a while he stops and makes a brief study of the fish, like a friend of mine who fished a bunch of worms one day and almost died of idleness because nothing happened. He knew exactly where the fish was lying, exactly how much line he had out and where the worms hung in the pool, although he didn't go to see them, and sat

171

waiting for the salmon to grow weary and finally take his offering. All at once he felt a knock. He held off for a moment or two and then lifted his rod point, but nothing happened. A short time after this the same thing happened and again, with reasonable pause in between, my friend lifted his rod and tried to hook his fish, but it was all quite useless. An hour passed and he decided to investigate. He propped the rod with a stick and crept down the side of the pool to discover that several salmon were hanging behind the worms swinging in the current. One after another they would advance, knock the worms with their snouts and then retreat again. The movement lifted the lead sinker from the bottom and let it fall again. The salmon were playing a game of their own.

What sort of a fish is the salmon? Those who fish for it will sometimes admit that the business requires a slight degree of skill and a much greater degree of luck. The salmon either runs or he doesn't. If he runs he comes fresh into the pool and he may be taken. If the freshet dies and the pool becomes stale, he sickens. If he stays long enough he becomes redder than the celebrated middle-cut, and if he stays too long he may get furunculosis when the drought really poisons the pool; but the fresh run fish is a wolf. The sea trout apart, there is nothing in the river with the same muscular power, the same drive to clear the falls and fight his way up the salmon ladder. Compared to the torpedo that is the clean salmon from the sea, the pike is a slow stupid fish. When the bright little spoon is drawn across the pool and the pike swirls to it, the experienced angler doesn't have to be told that he has hooked something inferior, no matter how fierce the pike may look. Watch the salmon come for the same spoon. He may not have the wicked snout of the pike, but he projects himself at the bait with a determination that can make a man's hackles rise just to see it, or induce such a trembling that a brandy flask will have to be brought out; yet the same fish may turn and swing back out again without taking the spoon or the devon. It will be a while, perhaps, before he can be irritated into making another dash.

Knowing the fish and its ways is as important as knowing the river in all its different aspects. Let the lure or the spoon hang for a moment and the salmon will turn away. The novice who doesn't understand the fish sometimes tries to let him catch the lure, forgetting that this is the powerful fish that came up through the flood, ploughed through the rocky gully and cleared the slabs below the pool. When he takes, he takes. Sometimes he is almost as gentle as a lamb and sometimes he is a wolf.

A friend of mine who has a great deal to do with stripping the fish when they are found in the feeder streams at the season's end and has been engaged in this work practically all his life, says that he has never been quite sure that a salmon won't take a bite at him one day. Watch the cock fish queueing at the redds and you will understand their wolfishness. The big fish drive off their rivals and if they don't feed in fresh water, they haven't forgotten how to bite one another. Their attacks are as vicious as those of strange dogs going for one another. Studying them, the keen salmon fisherman must admit that not only can they be full of fight and eager but they can also behave in a very odd way at weirs and in the entrances to minor rivers and streams in which they spawn. At one place not far from where I live the farmers would at a certain time of year band together to get themselves fish by beating the water and snatching whatever fish they could drive into the shallower ditches. The persecuted salmon could be induced to jump, squirm and wriggle until they could be tossed on to the bank with shovels and dung forks. They could be gaffed and occasionally taken out in a wrestling match if the would-be catcher of salmon didn't mind a wetting. Now and again some rash individual would try to take one by the tail, or gaff a monster too far back and find himself dragged into the river, for the salmon has the same muscular power in his body as may lie in an athlete's thigh muscles.

Not long ago I encountered a man who confessed that he had been tempted to strip and put on bathing trunks to take a salmon from a certain quiet pool on the river, since he had failed time and again to catch a fish there. Being a somewhat better swimmer than he was an angler, he managed to corner his fish, get his arms about it and stagger towards the bank. The fish, which he judged to be somewhere around the 15 lb. mark, seemed docile enough for a minute or two, but all at once it decided that it had been carried far enough and gave a single jerk of its body that almost took the poacher off his feet. He staggered, bruised his foot on a rock, and while he was trying to regain his balance the fish jumped in his arms, struck him heavily alongside the head and knocked him down. He saw no more of it after it regained the pool, but he wasn't in any shape to make a second attempt to capture it.

This sort of thing doesn't happen to the everyday, respectable salmon fisherman who knows the ways of the fish and the chances of taking one. I must admit that I am no salmon expert. The nature of salmon rivers and of salmon is something that requires a life-long study if one hopes to be a master of the art, as opposed to the sort of angler who comes and goes and waits for his limited technique to pay off. I would be a master if I had the ability and the time. This is my excuse, knowing there is a world of difference between the average angler and the master. What would I say the average angler needs? I fancy he would make a middling show with 40 per cent knowledge of the river and the ways of the fish, 10 per cent skill in fishing a spoon or a bait, and 50 per cent luck. He would be something more than an average angler if he knew all about the behaviour of salmon, and he would need far less luck.

Tools of the Villain's Trade

The very first salmon spear I ever saw was one in the process of manufacture on the blacksmith's anvil. I was a small boy at the time and I haunted the smithy. The blacksmith's son was making one or two tools for some local poachers. His father had made hundreds and there was nothing particularly furtive about the work. It wasn't illegal to make a spear, if it was against the law to be caught in the act using one. The worst that could have happened to the smith was that he might have lost a little of his estate business, for the riparian owners took a hard view of those who allied themselves with the poachers, but the spears were flounder spears, of course, and the smith couldn't be responsible if they were put to the wrong use! Last summer, when I was in that particular part of the world, the river keepers were having a fine old laugh to themselves. The self-same smith I had known as a boy had been taken on the river using one of his own spears and the great joke was that he had never attempted to take a salmon with a spear in his life before, although he had poached in other places for other sorts of game.

There appears to be a long tradition of mutual support between makers of this kind of tool and those who put them to use. In Wales generations of blacksmiths did a sideline business with generations of poachers. While many of the poachers were caught and ended in prison, the blacksmiths kept their noses clean. They were in the main content to take a few shillings or an occasional ill-gotten salmon as their reward.

There is something of a paradox in the fact that a poacher, well and truly taken in an offence, may end up with the fish. This may date from the day when there was no means of preserving fish and the magistrates decided that the fish itself needn't appear to pollute the atmosphere of the court. Some of the old country blacksmiths were the mainstay of the poachers' armoury, but here and there a quarry blacksmith kept his end up making spears, snatching hooks, barbed gaffs and so on. The conventional gaff has no barb, as every fisherman knows.

Poaching was rife long before the River Boards came on the scene, and when they did they had a daunting problem to discourage the worst offenders. Consider the temptation there was along the flashy rivers of mountain country. There were far fewer salmon ladders and passes than one sees today. The salmon sometimes filled the little rocky basins that marked the way to the headwaters and the spawning redds. Since a migrating salmon is about the most lithe, slippery and resilient creature that comes out of the water, only an optimist would attempt to grapple with one that has room to turn or lash its tail. The gaff or spear was a must for the successful poacher. In long runs the white treble hook —white because its colour made locating fish and hook a deal easier —was the favourite way of the foul-hooking villain.

In big pools a somewhat elaborate stroke-haul might be the choice. One that was popular at one time in a famous Scottish river consisted of a heavy iron bar of a length that allowed the use of several dozen hooks. The bar was trailed on a rope and the business was almost a local industry that took place while the law-abiding community looked the other way. Large-scale operations of this sort are unknown today, but not all snatchers, it must be whispered, are without permits and licences. Some have quite expensive equipment, including the best split-cane rods.

The crudest form of snatching is done with the barbed gaff, and bailiffs generally agree that where they take poachers with this sort of tool in their possession the implements are often antique. One of the crudest, and certainly a hand-me-down from a previous generation, is the take-down gaff. Weighing 20 lb. or more, and consisting of lengths of screwed iron piping, it gave the poacher a reach of about 9 ft. Quite plainly it had been made by a man who could screw a pipe and use a die, but he was certainly no great craftsman.

The apparently excessive weight had a purpose. The tool could be used in fast-flowing water and in deep water too. How many generations had used it no one could say, but the last man to try spent ten minutes or so assembling the monstrosity before stepping on to the rocks. He was as patient as his father had been, but he lost the family heirloom because times had changed. The bailiffs were telephoned when someone saw the poacher putting the tool together. When he looked up the snatcher saw that he had been too engrossed in getting a salmon for his own good. The long gaff fell into the hands of the authorities once and for all.

A collection of poaching ironmongery, confiscated some years ago, was displayed for my inspection on one occasion and I was able to identify the handiwork of one highly-skilled smith in the shape of three gaffs and hooks. Each had a similar rake and the barb was delicately fashioned. The scrolling of the hollow shanks to hold the binding cord was undeniably the work of one man, and I would have sworn that he had served an apprenticeship somewhere where higher skills were taught than in the local quarry workshops. An odd refinement on one of these gaffs was a razor-edged barb which marked it as an offensive weapon as well as a tool for snatching fish.

Spears, from what I have seen, were mainly of the flounder pattern, trident-shaped with a barb on each prong. Occasionally an improvising genius would take a small garden fork, make a saw cut in each prong, burn out the handle and drill a hole in the hollow shank so that the spear could be fastened to a pole or stout stick after the saw cut had been prised open to make a crude barb.

How many more poaching antiques lie in garden sheds and in dark understair cupboards to persuade the would-be salmon poacher to try his luck one day? The River Board can only wait until they turn up. Their biggest problem these days is probably illegal netting in the estuaries. This game is generally the work of gangs who watch the bailiffs as carefully as the bailiffs keep their eyes on the poachers. Sometimes the net comes up-river. Occasionally the poachers are taken in the act and fight their way out, and as often the River Board comes off best. The use of detonators and dynamite is far less frequent than it once was. Now and again a pool is poisoned. Burning the water is something that is written about in the folk-lore of Border poaching. Beating the water, an old Welsh pastime that needed a team to gaff and spear the fish in the ditches and feeders, also belongs in legend and the romantic aura has completely disappeared from the river poacher's image.

It isn't hard to understand. The river poacher was inclined to have sympathy when he plundered the fish that belonged to a privileged few. His crime today is no greater perhaps, but he is the recognised enemy of the general angling public. He is no longer a Robin Hood, and the truth is he never gave to the poor when he robbed the rich. His atavistic instincts prompted him to take fish by the first means that came to his hand and today the River Board copes with his sickness with remarkable efficiency, and little emotion, except perhaps when they think how much more severe the penalties should be, remembering those long-dead blacksmiths who left behind so many spears, gaffs and stroke-hauls.

Fishing on a Midsummer Night

Everything with mystery and mystique about it becomes more intriguing and fascinating when shrouded in shadows or covered by the night, and this explains to some degree why so many fishermen keep vigils on the sea trout pools when the world about them has gone to sleep. There was a time when it would never have entered my head to stay out all night fishing for a fish that could as easily be taken from the burn by day, but the burns I knew in my boyhood were comparatively deep and the fish in them had never been harried and disturbed by processions of fishermen going from pool to pool as they do by day on my local river. The salmon pools are bombarded with spoons, flies, worms and shrimps. The runs are trotted with tumbling baits and flashing silver lures until the sun goes down, and the salmon rest, but the wary sea trout lie in the holes beneath the trees, far down the undercut bank, out of the light, away from the procession of baits and the clump of the feet of the men plying their rods. The sea trout hardly moves at all until peace has returned to the water and the bank, until the sounds of children playing in the park have diminished, the long shadows are lining the water, the midges are rolling under the trees while the parr swim in the shallows along the shingle bank to the tail of the pool.

Last summer, when my leisure hours were inclined to be sporadic, I found it more convenient to run up the river and have a spell on one of the pools than make the longer journey to the lake. I am fonder of twilight fishing than I am of fishing in the dark, but when the river is low and the sea trout come up almost burrowing through the gravel, rolling, jumping and splashing with hardly enough water to cover their backs, it is better to be there in the dark. There is always a chance to lure one after it has won its way into the calm water, the glide where the pool hurries to pour itself out through the stones. The wait puts a strain on a man's patience, but wait one must. To go in too soon is to stand as a monument in the sight of the sea trout coming down to feed. The background of the sun-streaked sky is far too light. Sea trout coming up may be taken as they arrive, but those moving down to feed will come only so far and stay away thereafter if they see a fisherman aping the heron and standing in the water before the light has gone. It depends, of course, on how much a river is fished.

In general I find that an hour spent leaning on the wall contemplating the pool pays dividends even if one only studies the water's depth, the height to which a particular boulder or tree stump is submerged, the tendency for the level to rise or fall. This hour belongs to the bat. I hooked two last season when they flickered so close to the surface that they were either caught when the swimming fly encountered their wings or they actually tried to take the fly when I was in the act of lifting it. Things like that are hard to remember in sequence when one is concentrating on the imagined movement of a sea trout as it turns and swims effortlessly after the hurrying fly, following it like a dog until it begins to sweep right away in the faster water.

Before going in I look at the sky, judge the distance from the shallows on one side to the shallows on the other, the number of strides I may make in fishing the whole pool out in the thorough manner in which it should be fished, from the deeps where the downcoming fish turn and feed opposite the trees, to the vee where the last-minute take is indicated by a gentle knock and then the splash of the fish trying to make off with the hook in his jaw. I must be honest and say that sometimes I come just a little early because I want a particular pool to myself. I have been fishing it in imagination. I know how it will be when the air is cool and night is settled on the fields and the water is murmuring over the stones. Anyone else coming up and seeing me there will go on to the next pool, or take their turn behind me when the time comes. Most sea trout fishermen prefer to fish alone and have no one else to blame for failure if the take is missed or the water disturbed. The temperature being right and fish being prepared to move, it often happens that a good sea trout

178

shows in the pool long before I would begin to fish, but this is the essential discipline of the business, to hold off and reap the benefit of maximum cover.

Having scared one fish up the water, the rest that might come down will feed higher up and one must then wait for the incomers if there are any moving upriver. I like to wade in when I can just see the bushes on the far bank and measure my first cast so that I can keep that length of line, casting a little up, keeping control and maintaining contact with the fly, making a short hand recovery if needed, but not really working the fly back until it is directly below me. The taking arc seems to be most frequently within forty-five degrees of the directly downriver position.

No one works a sea trout fly in quite the same way as the next man, it seems, but then no one wades to the same depth, uses the same line and the same fly on the end of the same sort of cast. On some nights the sinking line and the heavy fly seem to be necessary. This may be because the water is in a particularly dead state, the fish are moving even in the shallows, at a particular depth, or see only those objects floating so many inches from the surface. On other nights the sinking line is a drag. It seems to scare the fish, disturb the water when it is lifted. The old hand gets out his gut cast or ties on a gut collar between his line and the everyday nylon cast. This is a compromise. Fishing in the dark one sees so little. There are so many handicaps that experimentation bedevils judgement altogether. The fish take half-heartedly, or do they? The gentle tug at the end of the pool could have been the hook encountering stone or weed. After a few casts one gingerly recovers the line and the fly and finds that the barb of the hook has gone, but when did it go? Did it break an hour back? The eager fisherman knows he should have checked the barb with regularity in a place with so many slabs of rock cluttering the run, and now the fly has to be changed.

To change a cast in midstream is not too difficult but things may fall from one's pocket and if the change cannot be made without the aid of a torch one must plod back to the shingle and perform the task sheltering the light from the reflecting surface of the pool as much as one can. Who hasn't come to that moment and found that the torch wouldn't light or, worse still, is lying in the car?

People down in the town may be suffering from insomnia and sigh to hear the church clock chiming, but the night is never really long enough when one finds that now the fly is firmly hooked in a branch of a tree. The frustrations of night fishing try a man's sanity, and yet there is that moment when it happens, the good hard tug of a greedily taking sea trout, the wild plunging and splashing that comes before the moment

179

when one must hold steady and feel for the net slung on one's shoulder.

This is the climax of the vigil, the daydream enjoyed under the oak tree when woodsmoke was drifting across the field, the long spell of careful casting and recovering, the ritual working of the fly, upwards, now across, now down to the tail. The average sea trout may be two or three pounds. For a minute the taking fish is five or six, or more, and then it doesn't really matter. It is bright and silvery, swirling, tugging, swimming in a sort of marking-time desperation as the net gets dipped, the rodpoint swayed in a half circle, the fish brought over the frame and scooped out as one walks backwards to the strand. There are people lying abed who never dreamt of things like this, weary men who might be more refreshed by the experience than by a whole night sleeping the sleep of the dead.

Fishing in Coloured Water

The stream was clear enough when I got to it, but I knew there was something wrong about the conditions. Flies tumbled about in the shelter of bushes, but no fish rose, except those tireless fingerlings that are to be found in shallow runs. They feed because they must, it always seems, and they very rarely take a rest. I knew what it was half an hour later, that feeling of things not being right, for a single drop of cool rain fell on my fist as I was casting. We were in for a downpour. In five minutes or so it came. The water was broken by spearing raindrops that seemed to sprout from it like a thick bed of round rushes. The colour didn't come at once. It never does, for it first of all fills in the puddle holes at the cattle drinking places and washes down banks and shallow waterways, and even then the fluid mud hangs in the backwaters and eddies.

It is a while before the change comes and one begins to see that colour is on the way. If the stream has peaty ditches and feeders the water carries tiny fragments of moss and peat and the colour is slow in showing. Instead of the brown of a clay wash one notices a sort of dark beer tint, and then the brew thickens until the bottom can hardly be seen. Everything is screened by the flow of solids transported by the increasing flood.

Upstream of me was a fairly long stretch of broken bank where cattle would stand in the evening quenching their thirst, and soiling the stones.

I knew that long before the real colour came it would be quite futile to fish the fly.

The fish could taste the pollution, and if they had any inclination to feed it would disappear until they got the flood that carried grubs and worms washed out of the minor streams and those deposits of dead leaves below the hedges. I reeled in and went up the bank. I had had enough, what with branches filtering water down my neck and the occasional cold drop of rain rolling off the peak of my 'twa-snooted' bonnet, as the stylishly dressed young salesman had called my choice of fishing hat when I bought it 10 or 15 years before.

I took refuge in a building up among the trees and presently I was joined by a forestry worker. He looked down at the stream and said it would soon be at its best. He was a worm fisherman. He reminded me of the blacksmith of my boyhood, and he had been like the wild duck, for he loved nothing better than a wet night. Let it rain until he was wet all the way up to his armpits, he would still toss a worm into the flooded burn.

We had fished together dozens of times, wandering on and on into the back of the moor with the sky getting lower and lower and the sound of the burn in spate drowning our infrequent exchanges of information. We caught a lot of good 'burnies' as we called them. Once we had some wonderful sea-trouting going down the burn until we met the river. The worm could not be beaten, the smith said. I thought about that when the forestry man reached into his pocket and brought out a tin. It contained worms and moss.

How much one changes over the years. Once, my thanks would have been quite spontaneous, but now, I suppose, I have a subconscious feeling that there is something not quite right about fishing with worm. I took them and said I would leave them under a stone. I didn't suppose I would stay long and my benefactor would be sure of having a few for his fishing later on.

It took me a while to rig up a tackle. I wasn't really equipped for the business. What I needed was that long-ago spruce pole, a length of brown line and a hook to gut, but I managed. Soon I was down on the coloured water, standing in the rain, letting the flood swirl round my feet while I waited for something to take the worm as it trundled into the undercut bank, lost in the thick soup of the flood. Something did take it, a trout of perhaps ¾ lb. Where it had come from I could not imagine. Certainly when the water had been clear there had been no sign of that sort of fish in the locality, but then I thought of long-gone days again and the way trout live in long, underwater caverns that lie beneath rocks protruding from the bank. All at once I was fishing with enthusiasm, for I could imagine bigger trout rising than ever came at the fly; trout that even the night-fishing heron never saw; trout that only came out into the coloured water of the spate. I didn't notice the rain going up my sleeves, but I got it over my boots once or twice and found the sudden immersion a bit of a shock. I caught two more trout and twice lost a worm on a bramble bush on the far side, reminding myself that once I could have lobbed a worm into the turning water with wonderful precision and knowing just how it would swing along the bank as the current took it.

Down beyond a particularly brown boil of water there was a slowly-turning pool. Here, when I managed to put the worm in at the right spot, I suddenly felt a good, heavy tug. The rod tip went down. I reminded myself of something more relevant than the way to fish a worm, the fact that good split cane flyrods should be treated with respect, and not used for anything so crude as throwing a worm into a muddy flood. I did not get the big one. He went off with the worm and the hook.

I had three fish I could not have taken with a fly. I put the tin of worms under the stone as I had promised, leaving half-a-crown in with them so that the forestry man could buy himself a drink. The colour was on for the night. I could see that, although the woods all around were hazed and almost completely obscured by the steady downpour of rain.

Fishing From the Shore

There was a time, I remember my father telling me, when Sir Herbert Maxwell fished from the shore at Monreith, in Wigtownshire, not in quite the manner one might have expected from such a distinguished authority on salmon fishing, but, with the aid of his keepers, using a net. He was after salmon, and perhaps sea trout that came into the mouth of the burn there. Small boys who hung about, as my father did, contrived to get within the arc of the net and put down their feet on a flounder that, if the keeper, or Sir Herbert happened to be in a good humour, they were allowed to lift before moving out of the way. My father enjoyed this, but he was fonder of fishing for John Dory, a small fish often caught there or from one of the points close to the village.

For all that my father wasn't a fisherman at heart, any more than his father was. Both of them fished exclusively for the pot. They had little time to stand and stare, for they were essentially practical. I need hardly say that it was otherwise with me. I liked the long strand and the summer haze of salt air. I loved the rocky inlets and the wrack-draped cliff bottoms. I could see all kinds of fish in the green depths, some of them real and some imaginary. A flounder has a beauty of its own as it glides across a stretch of fine gravel. There is nothing more breath-taking than a full-bodied bass seen nosing in at some cleft in the rock.

When there were no fish or I had done dreaming about them, there was the Atlantic storm debris, washed in by the Irish coast and the Mull of Galloway, to end up, rock-ground, sand-polished smooth as a knee bone, on the deserted shore. I suppose it was the hypnotic quality of this kind of scene that made me a shore fisherman, but it took time. I had to fish the burns and the lochs, and go away and come back again, before I caught a bass—farther north in the warm Drift current than I had been led to believe they went, until I took one.

The thing about fishing in the sea is the mystery of what it may produce according to the state of the tide and the weather. It can be a broad wilderness with nothing moving right down to the dark shadows of the deeps. It can also be an enchanted world of swaying weed with travelling fry of one sort of another: whitebait, sandeels, school bass, mackerel, rock-hugging wrasse, or fat mullet with faces like the ghost of the village policeman. I didn't take to the shore until I came to rest in this part of the world, and then I went fishing with a salmon threadline outfit upon which the locals, who had never seen anything so far out and unlikely, smiled their scorn.

I was ahead of my time. I was also extravagantly careless of the effect of salt water on such a delicate mechanism as a fixed-spool reel. At that time all fixed-spool reels were expensive. The revolution hadn't happened. I often feel sorry that it ever did, for now the journey to the remote cove is longer. Now the shingle is camped upon by a motley crowd of anglers, some skilled and some not so skilled. Many of the fraternity only know that the fish begin to feed an hour or so before the tide is at its peak and an hour afterwards. They have no conception of the movement of fish, one species hunting another, smaller one, plankton attracting fry and sandeels, and bigger fish patrolling to trap a shoal in some bay or inlet.

What does a man do when, standing all alone, on the most remote estuary, bass swim within two or three feet of his thighs without once bothering to turn at the vibrating, swaying silver spoon or the whirling spinner? How does he lure the mullet that flash away at the slightest movement on his part, and then, with the passing of time, materialise

183

again, grey shapes like a reconnaissance party working its way over the hills and across the valleys of submerged sandbanks? No matter what the majority of shore fisherman angle for, I fish to be there and to have an excuse for it all. I love to try my hand, fishing deep for a big mackerel perhaps, or skittering a small lure at times half out of the water just to see something big swirl at it and carry it away with the brute strength of the virile bass.

And then there is the business of fishing for shark—the tope or dogfish- which can be done from at least one shore not many miles from my door. How the rod vibrates, even when the taker is only a dogfish. What a lovely thing is the spotted dog with his skin a replica of the mottling of a gravel bed from which he has been lifted, his tail swiping and slapping as he tries to get away and his baleful shark eyes looking at the world above the water.

First one must go and catch a whiting to bait the line for such a monster. The whiting is a fish for the cat, an unexciting lump that pleases the man with a stomach ulcer as much as it pleases the idling tope before he prods it again and then, sweeping round, carries it away in his jaws on his first wild run.

All this is crude when compared with the delicate business of the dry fly. Finesse is a word not often used about shore fishing except, perhaps, when a small float, or no float at all, is employed and small pieces of fat on the tiniest hook are offered to the browsing mullet. Mullet may take fat in the 'hailstorm' of fragments washed downstream from inland villages and sewage outflows. One can, however, try the salmon fly and the floating line, though this is less productive than fishing feathers for such fish as bass, mackerel or pollack. One does it hoping that some wayward salmon or sea trout, off course on his way to the river, may come at the fly and hook himself. To be honest, I think the summer bass, however he is taken, with a tiny lure or a big, erratically darting spoon, fights better than any fresh-run salmon, but, then, he is a coarser fish and more of a hobble-de-hoy altogether. His flesh isn't the delicate flesh of the sea trout, nor the flaking delight of the newly-boiled salmon, but the seaside landladies used to colour him up with cochineal and call him rock salmon on their menus.

There is a time for everything. The shore fisherman learns this as the years pass. He knows that bass come in late May or June and the bigger shoals of mackerel in July and early August. He sees the mullet in the oily stillness of slack water on a warm evening in August and stirs the jumble in his tackle box for finer and finer items, lead shot like dust, gilt hooks fit for the most fastidious, shy roach. In a few weeks it is over. The warm currents have diminished and the jellyfish no longer come sailing in, jostling one another, it would seem, to get into the thickest plankton soup. The gulls gather far out where a shoal of silver fish dance, but these are the stragglers. The bass, if they are there, have gone from the surface to feed deeper.

They fell victim to the fisherman with the flagpole rod and the outsize multiplier reel who casts his huge weights to the very horizon and then squats down to smoke and contemplate the slow progress of a heavily-laden tanker on its way across the bay.

I never go to the shore so late on. The magic has gone by then. The migrants linger here and there, but they know, as well as the man who fishes the summer tides, that what brought them and sustained them day after day in summer is no longer to be found.

Nymph and Shepherd

The late Oliver Kite, who wrote the best book on nymph fishing I have ever read, removed some of the inhibitions I had hitherto cultivated with regard to nymph fishing, but to be truthful I always felt that imitating a nymph, while it may be less difficult than tying an imitation of the natural fly, is, from the point of view of fishing technique, the most difficult thing about the whole business.

I didn't discover the nymph after I read about it. I discovered the nymph long, long ago, lying full length and getting my midriff wet, while I watched one rising out of the depths of a green, gravelly pool of the burn. Here, I told myself, is the thing the green and gold trout sucks in just before he breaks the surface. Here is the thing that is like the little fly that no one can imitate, the Curse that makes a tidal debris of corpses when the hatch is over, like it not because it is too small or too difficult to copy, but because it moves jerkily, almost vertically in the water. It then holds off for a minute or two, its wing cases breaking as it becomes an imago and a hatching fly.

I have tied hundreds of nymphs and used only a few. The essential thing about fly-fishing is faith. One has faith if the experiment works, even once. The conviction grows with time and circumstance, and nymph fishing, which some people hold is simply wet-fly fishing when the fly is anything but a lure or a beetle, was a business I didn't turn to except as a last resort. After all, Kite fished the chalk stream and was a fanatic trout fisherman. I do not think he was quite so addicted to the wilder lakes or the big reservoirs, and I have been obsessed with lakes and wild places for the greater part of my fishing life. On the lake a lure fished deep produces results even in summer. Often, when the algae is thick as soup, and there is no widespread hatch of fly, the lure is the only remedy, but there are times when fish are feeding and neither the deep-fished lure nor the fly on the surface, gently drifted across the bays, produces a noticeable result. One tries everything and anything. Analysing what makes me a fly-fisherman I would not say it was the bag I make, or even the size of the fish I catch, but the challenge of the whole thing. It began that way and I suppose it will end that way.

The problem is a present one, one that I face every time I sally forth, and if I do not win I study why I have failed. I did this long ago on the burns. I caught particular trout, a fish that lived under a slab bridge of old railway sleepers, one that moored himself behind a rock in a cutting that drained a loch, another that had a hole below a land drain leading into the burn. Even in lakes and lochs one gets to know that a certain fish rises in a certain place. It has its territory between two water marks, two sunken rocks or boulders or the lee side of a defile of slate, and it rises there again and again, season after season, if it is a fish worth catching. In a season it gains weight. In a season one learns that it wins because of the way it comes up and goes down or the sort of thing it goes for. A good fish only becomes a challenge by the frequency with which it defeats its enemies in their skilled efforts to lure it to take the fly—or nymph.

I had fished this particular lake more than once without a great deal of success. In its early days there were stories of wonderful trout grown large on rich feeding, for a reservoir had been formed by flooding a valley and drowning a village or several small settlements, a thing that happens in Wales from time to time. I was fishing on this particular day in the month of June. The weather had not been kind until then, but all at once it was too kind, and the lake, instead of having foam on the far shore, had a gentle ripple. Although I could not see any fish rising to a fly I knew they were feeding because every so often the dimples broke the even ripple. Every fisherman of any experience at all knows the nymphing fish. Some, and my long-ago instructor, the country joiner, was one, say that it is a waste of time to bother with nymphing fish. It is as fastidious as the chalkstream trout taking the spinner. It will not have anything that does not look just like the thing that has stimulated its appetite. Go home, say the closed minds, and come back when the trout mean what they are doing and not fooling.

186

When I travel 40 miles to fish, and I often do, I don't like to give up easily. The challenge is a little greater. I owe it to myself to fish hard or I become introvert, considering if I really am a dedicated fisherman, or whether I am a very poor sportsman and a man who gives in. On this occasion I was on the verge of giving in when a man suddenly appeared over a hillock behind me. He had two dogs with him and a hazel crook in his hand. The handle of the crook, I noticed when he came closer, was carved from bone or the horn of a ram. It was in the shape of a leaping fish. I paused and admitted my lack of success. The shepherd looked across the lake. He had the far-away look of men of his calling who search the landscape for missing ewes. It was not much of an evening, but still the cuckoo called and it was not too late in the month to catch good trout if one offered the right thing.

He looked in my flybox and pointed at the nymphs, the smallest of them. A lake is always 1,000 times wider than a burn, a stream, or even a river. It is a vast sea into which to cast a very small thing like a nymph, made from two or three strands of peacock herl or a bit of pheasant tail. One becomes used to scaling down the fly from one lake size to another, but some nymphs are not much bigger than midges and it was to these that the shepherd's stubby finger pointed. I had to put them on my cast. It took me several minutes. By that time the shepherd was away, his dogs ranging through the heather to which he had walked, and an old ewe bouncing before him.

The nymphs went down with the slightest disturbance. I remembered how they should work, like the nymph in the burn coming up to break the surface. I was full of book-learning, of course, but it all harked back to seeing a hatching fly, and so I let the ripple work the fine cast and made the retrieve as gentle as I could, imagining the nymph, the natural, living insect, rising in the water. Suddenly there it was, a slightly below-the-surface take, a good pull down, and a fish making the line go like a grocer's cheese-cutting wire.

I have no conceit of myself so far as knowledge is concerned, but I take a pride in being able to follow what I have been taught. I had hooked my fish knowing the way to work the nymph. I had made it take because the shepherd had pressed me to see what I had seen and ignored, that the fish were nymphing, and he knew that the size was important. I brought the fish back. It boiled once and went down again, but it couldn't stand the continual strain of being pumped up. At last it came sideways over the net, undone by the use of a nymph. Oliver Kite would have approved. He might even have shaken his head that I needed a Welsh shepherd to tell me what to do. The second fish took in exactly the same way, and the third confirmed that I had not been mistaken about what to do, or how to do it.

I had had enough. I stopped. The shepherd, I noticed, was away up the slope on the far side of the lake, plodding on and his dogs flowing up and down over the short-cropped grass as sheep dogs do.

Gone Fishing

I might have missed all the joys of fishing had the smithy not been there beside the burn. The smith and his sons taught me how to catch a trout, if not with the fly, with the 'garden fly'—the worm. They taught me early and never knew how thoroughly they had inoculated me with the disease until one of the last of that family, whom I met after a lapse of fifty years, recalled his father setting me up with tackle when I was supposed to be at school.

That day I had caught the bug, but my first real excursion up the burn came a little later when, excused from attending the school, I took a message to the smith about something needing doing at the farm. The smith and his three grown sons lived a tempestuous life. They were all good men at their trade. They all had their own ways of doing things and they were often at cross purposes. When the forge became too hot to hold them all, one of them would go off to the town in a temper to drink whisky. One went fishing and the remaining son would wait upon his father, muttering curses.

The one who went fishing was Willie. His temper cooled quickest, and I think he sometimes started the trouble because the burn was in spate. He could tell that it was by the roar from under the bridge or the rattling of the waterwheel.

My first proper excursion with Willie wasn't planned. I just got in the way, as I must often have done. The sparks were flying. Recriminations ricochetted from the black rafters where the iron was stacked, and Willie, the fisherman, threw down his hammer and said he was finished. He damned them all to a hotter place, and turning, knocked me down. He wasn't a bad man, Willie. He picked me up again and said he was sorry. If I liked he would take me fishing. I followed Willie out to the garden where he dug worms for me, gave me a tobacco tin to keep them in, and a rod and line to fish with.

Half an hour after he had shown me where to drop the worm I knew

188

the throbbing and bending of the rod with more than the force of the current and a fish at the end of my line! I had caught my first really big slippery trout. It was a picturebook fish, green on the back, yellow beneath. It had bright red spots, and no fear in its eye as I tried to get it off the hook. I held on to it for dear life. Twice it almost slipped out of my hand. I put it up on the grass in the shelter of the bracken and covered it with a stone. I was in a dilemma whether to rush off home with it or stay and catch another. Willie had demonstrated the way to put a worm on the hook but this took me a long time. When I looked for him to see if everything was in order I saw his bobbing figure moving far up the burn.

Willie didn't come back to ask how I was getting on. A man caught fish with his line in the water. He hardly ever caught anything talking about it. I caught another trout, a better one than the first, half an hour later, but this one jumped and tugged and broke away when I staggered and almost fell trying to get him out, and I made up my mind to be more circumspect the next time the line began to cut the water. I had got the hang of putting the worm on the hook. I began to think where I would swim if I were a fish.

A third trout braced the line and made the rod bend, and this one I fought out of his element, over a submerged stone and into the shallows. I slipped and got the seat of my trousers wet, but what did that matter? I had two handsome trout. I would soon have a dozen if my worms lasted. If they didn't I would squelch away down to the smithy and the potato patch and dig some more. This was the thing I was going to do forever. It didn't occur to me that before the big trout came out of their holes under the rocks, there had to be a spate and a lot of colour in the water. I looked at the sky. It would soon be night.

When at last I went home I had seven sizeable trout. The worms had all gone. I discovered that I was hungry and cold. To tell the truth, water ran out of my clothes when I stood still. They were not impressed with me at home. All at once I was standing stark naked in front of a fire, wrapped in a towel while water was boiled for the tub. I was dosed with toddy, and no one gave my trout a second glance. Willie's idleness was talked about. Bullocks had been carried away by that burn in spate. Ricks had even been floated when it overflowed. Disasters, or the thought of them, left the family open-mouthed in horror. What would my father have said had he known the danger I was in that day? What would he say if I caught my death of pneumonia?

The seven trout lost their brilliance, as trout left on a plate soon do. In the morning they seem to have shrunk, and they never appeared on the table. The company of cats that always sat warming themselves in the hearth had them for dinner, and I was left to my secret dreams of catching trout with worms as soon as I could escape again. It went on that way, I must confess, for most of my life. The only thing that changed was that I gave up forking the garden for worms and took to catching my fish with the fly, but I know when it all happened, the way some boys remember the first time they scored a goal or hit a six. It was pure magic.